T0128213

**Also by Anne Austin**

A Feather, Falling
Rainbows in the Snow
Archie and Arthur, a Mouse's Tale
Strategies of Survival
A Viable Alternative
Cherries on the Cake

# CIRCLES
## WITHIN
# CIRCLES
## THE LIFE OF A SEER

### D. ANNE AUSTIN

Order this book online at www.trafford.com
or email orders@trafford.com

Most Trafford titles are also available at major online book retailers.

Print information available on the last page.

ISBN: 978-1-6987-0101-1 (sc)
ISBN: 978-1-6987-0100-4 (e)

*Trafford rev. 04/28/2020*

 www.trafford.com

**North America & international**
toll-free: 1 888 232 4444 (USA & Canada)
fax: 812 355 4082

FOR MY GRANDMOTHER, ANNE GAVIN, A SEER

Cyprus 1st April 2020

## CIRCLES WITHIN CIRCLES, THE LIFE OF A SEER

### CYCLES WITHIN CYCLES

This book is for everyone who is born with the gifts of the seer and who needs a friend to help him or her, understand why they see differently, hear differently and sense differently. Maybe you won't have anyone in the family who can help you. So this book is written with love to help take away the isolation and the fear. The often terrifying nightmares, where you are accessing past recall, revisiting the Akashic records and having in a way, a spiritual Ph.D. when asleep, and reverting to the life of a four year old at school, learning to read and count when awake. That is tough! Everything is from my own experience which I share with you. With love, humour and compassion.

If you were born into a family of seers, as I was, you will carry these gifts in your blood line, maybe for many generations, they were healers, seers, dreamers. musicians, 'sensitive,' is the collective name for all of these categories of people. A psionic analysis of a drop of your blood or a hair of your head, a witness they are called, will show the extent of your gifts. Homeopathy uses a witness to see where your ancestors had a weakness, perhaps in their chest and these are called miasms. In families, gifts are usually carried down the female line. In Celtic cultures there is s strong tradition of families who were known to have the' gifts. 'Sometimes called the 'Sixth Sense,' or being 'fey.'. I think this word is derived from, 'fairy.'

A tradition in Scotland was to put a Lucken booth brooch, or carving, beside a newly born baby so that the fairies could not exchange one of their own kind with a mortal child. Since I am of Celtic blood, an Irish citizen by descent through my grandmothers, as well as being a Scot by birth, the traditions of both countries resonate.

I am called after my maternal grandmother, a seventh child of a seventh child. There is a worldwide belief that such children possess extra sensory perception. Perhaps that is why we love fantasy so much!

'Superman,' 'Spiderman,' Batman' and all the others. They strike a chord!

Mythology, half god, half man affects us in the same way. We feel at ease, at one, with the myths, fables and legends of Ancient Greece and Scandinavia almost to the extent that they are our reality, not that which we are born into. So the feeling of alienation from others who don't see as we do can lead to loneliness. My maternal grandmother was a remarkable medium and clairvoyant but it was hushed up by the family. I wish I had known her. She would have understood and helped me as a little girl, seeing angels, spirits, children who 'weren't there,' in broad daylight, crying so sadly on a bitterly cold winter's day, barefoot and in pyjamas. in the snow. When I ran home to tell my mother, she was frightened, obviously seeing her mother's gifts in me and I was told, like all of us are, that it was a figment of my imagination! Still as vivid today as it was when I was six years old. My male cousins from that side of the family also had experiences which I understand now. One, seeing a boy with a gun in a remote farmhouse in Perthshire who was the late son of the family. Another came out of his body during Yoga, his first lesson and he never went back. Astral projection, like that, is a rare accomplishment but he didn't want to open that door!

In my own four children, I see the gifts of creativity and sensitivity. Their choice, of course, if they wish to openly bring forward their spiritual gifts. Great kind and good people, humorists!

There are two other aspects which are definitely a part of a young child's life when they are very open. Intuitive faculties manifest and it is almost impossible for a seer not to tell the truth. Of course that leads to trouble at times when we are told to be less forthcoming and to be diplomatic! We 'see through' people with the greatest of ease. It is impossible to fool a seer. Luckily, we seem to have a strong personal ethic, even as small children to adhere always to the truth and never to abuse the gifts we have been born with.

Since we all have a Guardian angel who is with us, always, throughout our life we are safe and simply have to invoke them when we are afraid. Prayer is different from Invocation.

Prayer makes the connection with spirit and is usually in praise. Invocation is inviting help, when we need it. Just as we would not go to a wedding or a party without an invitation, the saints and goddesses will not enter our life without us asking them in. They would be bypassing our will which is not permitted. We use simple language that a small child will understand, for example, 'Virgin Mary, help me now.' Or,' Goddess KwanYin, help me now.'

And remember to say "Thank you!'

When you utter those words, the grace that will help you floods into your life. It's like a spiritual bank account and if we don't utilize it, what a waste!

So, let's imagine that you have now grown to around ten or eleven years old. That's when the intellectual processes kick in and you may think your gifts are fading away, but no, they simply go into the background of your life for a time, rather like a weaving with work going on smoothly behind the foreground. Sport, after school activities, hormones kicking in, take pride of place. but the higher gifts are always there, popping up when you don't expect them.

Your intuition will be as alert as ever. As you chat in a group you may feel uncomfortable about someone, superficially nice and friendly, but why does your solar plexus feel odd?

That is the true brain of the body. Our physical brain is all about Logic, Maths, Physics but if we get information in our "gut," that's the one to follow, always.

As a seer you will pick up energies in a variety of ways. It might be though our sense of sight, might be though our sense of sound, might be through our sense of touch or our sense of smell. There is no better or worse than. If you are strongest with vision then hearing and touch etc will soon follow.

You might visit a friend's home and immediately you feel ill at ease. The parents may have been arguing before you got there and the vibrations will still be tangible for you to pick up with your, 'antennae, 'as it were.

Or you may feel there's a certain part of town that isn't a good place for you to be. That could be sensitivity to something that has happened there, or you have a premonition, a warning, to leave the place. This often is the case of people who decide not to fly because they have an uneasy feeling in the solar plexus and they learn later the plane had an accident.

When we have this awareness it can be difficult to explain to others why we make certain decisions. I have found that if I am in extreme danger, I hear my guides speak clearly, just behind my right ear. Just as clearly as someone calling you to come home.

The words are few. 'Run now!' 'It's not your time!' 'Go back!'

When my guides communicate with me ordinarily, it is telepathically and visually combined.

As if there is an extra crystalline lens? Half way between the eye and the ear, sight and sound, in combination.

I think it will be the left ear for seers who are right handed. Being left handed, I get migraines at the right hand side of my head and I hear the guides speak at my right ear.

A healer told me she was running away from the tsunami in Thailand. Everyone was running along the beach She heard her guide's voice, clearly saying," Climb!" She grabbed her husband by the arm, climbed a cliff and they survived. Sadly, the others did not. So voices in the head are normal for us. As are warning signs from the solar plexus, reading the vibrations of people and places.

One of the most important things to remember as a sensitive is that we can fool ourselves. If we try to use the gifts for ourselves, it won't work doesn't stop us trying though! Until we realize that whenever we try, we get wrong results, then we accept the truth. We are here in service to others. That is our Life Path, our true Destiny. If we could use them for ourselves, we would have an unfair advantage over others. None of us wants to be a masochist after all! There has to be a level playing field. In fact, if you were to know the story of seer's, clairvoyants', mediums' lives, call us what you will, they would have remarkable stories to tell, of insurmountable challenges, but they came through them. Somehow, with FAITH.

When we realize there are others like us, it is euphoric! We don't need to persuade anyone of the truth of what we see, because they see it too!. We have a great kind of visionaries' vocabulary which transcends words. There's a brotherhood or sisterhood at work. If one's in trouble then another will help, all knowing that no matter how accurately we see for others, not for ourselves. So we trust each other as we would a family member, for that truly is the way it is.(This almost feels like the esprit de corps of the Military.)

TRUST is hugely important in the work of the seer. You will be tested again and again and again. In the beginning of your work you will hear, as you channel, your guide's voice. Before you begin your session, address an audience, do platform work or however you wish to bring out your gifts, say the words., either orally or mentally, 'I WORK IN LIGHT, LOVE AND TRUTH. PLEASE PROTECT US.'

There, you have said it. You have set your INTENTION.

Here are some examples of the challenges you will face.

Someone comes to see you a beautiful, talented woman. An artist with exhibitions in New York and London, polished, cosmopolitan and wealthy.

And you open the faculty and what comes across would fit the life of the victim of the Mafia.

Terror, cruelty, fear for her life.

At the end, I hung my head in embarrassment and said these words.

'1 am so sorry. I must have got things so badly wrong.'

She looked at me, wiping away tears and said,

'That was exactly true. No one has ever heard my story.'

From that moment, I told my guides I would never doubt what they tell me, regardless of what my 'ordinary 'eyes might tell me.

You may well be asked to help family members. A lot of seers won't do this for family, because they can't be sure of their impartiality. Personally, I think if you use those words given, love will help you to be accurate.

If you are asked a huge question in the person's life, like' Should I leave Shanghai and go to work in Los Angeles?' and they are told 'No' but they really want to do it, advise them to check out with another two seers. This went ahead and as predicted ended unsuccessfully, sadly. People often don't get what they want to hear but we are dealing with truth, not diplomacy!

This was an examples of common sense. not being used. We all know that working in the USA needs a green card which can take years after applying and do we have any contacts there to help? Being spiritual does not mean we give up on common sense. There are so many examples of this,' My guides told me I have to do this.'

As soon as our own desires colour what we want, clarity simply disappears! I think this is a good guide. If we strongly are asked by spirit to do something and our personality self-rejects it completely out of fear, then we know it is genuinely coming from them, if the pressure continues. For me it feels like two violet hands pushing me forward and the pressure doesn't stop till I have sent the message or made the phone call.

When the inner turbulence subsides then I know, as the carrier, I have done my work.

We have mentioned that being a seer often comes from the family line It can also come by means of an accident to the head, or in one case a childhood eye injury brought forward amazing spiritual art. This would also be with the soul's acceptance.

Before we reincarnate the soul goes to a meeting of wiser, more enlightened beings.

There, the match, as to the family that would afford us the best incarnation for the lessons that our soul needs for its progress, is consented to, or not. By us. If, for example, we felt it would be too difficult to cope with being an athlete and losing the power of our physical body through a degenerative disease, we might say, 'no'. Then we go back into the Inner Planes to wait for a better match. Our will dictates. This is very helpful for people to know, if, for example, they are divorcing and worried about the effect on their children's lives. The soul would have seen this and accepted it as would the souls of their children have accepted that their parents would divorce or they would not have come back into that family group.

This takes us into the realm of Predestination, Fate and Destiny. Let's imagine a sandwich made up of three layers. The top layer is a rough outline of our life plan It can't be too exact or it would take away our own freewill to make choices.

The filling of the sandwich comprises the bombshells that challenge us in our life, usually at the Emotional plane level, for that plane is where we grow most in life.

We may experience the loss of a parent at an early age.

It may be that a virus disrupts the life of the planet, as of now.

Our firm may have been taken over by a larger firm.

We may have married a gambler who makes us homeless.

And so on.

These bombshells are Fate.

We have no control over them.

But we have control over Destiny, our third layer of the sandwich.

Here is an example. An elderly, sweet, old lady came to visit at New Year in Scotland, with a basket containing sherry for me and whisky for my husband ; pouring a glass for each of us, to wish us' Happy New Year.'

Then in my twenties, I innocently asked her if she had gone to the kirk, (church,) that day which was the custom then Scotland celebrated New Year more than Christmas, and children in the Highlands got their gifts on that day.

The sweet old lady vanished before my eyes, becoming filled with anger as she said,

'I will never go into a kirk again! He gave my Johnnie when we were sixteen to the sea.

And I will never forgive Him!' Johnnie was her love and a fisherman.

That's Destiny. Do we accept what Fate has given us as a trial or reject it? Probably stopping our growth. Positive or negative reaction.

Great love and great hate pull us magnetically back to the other soul, lifetime after lifetime. If we don't want this to happen, then feeling nothing at the time of our passing will stop the process. Like a pendulum that swings from side to side and rests tranquilly in the middle, motionless.

Earlier I have written that children are very open when they are tiny, seeing angels, and orbs and family members who have passed, guarding them.

When our spiritual selves really open to their fullness it can be a shock, the Kundalini force rising in the spine, perhaps because of a soul connection returning, and activating the two channels on either side of the spine. One may have been dormant but now wakens and shocks the system till the heightened vibrations settle. Polarity at work.

Science and Spirituality go hand in hand, always to the same truth in the end. Einstein knew this. Spiritual people usually get there before scientists. The knowledge of time and the lopsided view of linear time is an example, when emotional time is quite different. Compare our enjoyment of a candlelit meal with the beloved and our time in the dentist's waiting room!

Some people, seers are open all the time. The gifts never switch off. They seldom sleep much and day and night run into each other. Others choose when they will use the gifts and when they will close them down. Remember, you are in charge. Suppose you are driving and you find yourself drifting to a higher level, very easily done Then you address the guides who want to communicate and tell them,' Not now, while I am driving, later, yes.' That is really important for everyone's safety.

Here are some ways where you can break the connection from the spiritual plane to the material plane.

If you are finishing a healing or seeing session, both sides of the same coin, run cold water over the insides of your wrists for a minute or two. Each seer is a healer and the reverse is true. Just like water, hot or cold. When giving out healing, some will perceive it as hot, others as cold, depending on their own polarity. Back to Physics again.

If you have been doing a lot of spiritual work, place the index finger between the eyebrows lightly, with your dominant hand. Place thumb and middle finger on each side of the bony part of your nose to make a triangle. Again, very gently, hold that position for about ten seconds till you feel aware fully of the world around you and lift the fingers away.

If there is a concentration of too much energy in the head, go to a quiet place where no one will observe you snapping ur fingers vigorously around your head. That breaks up the accumulation of too much power.

To close the chakras, stand up straight and with the right hand make a scooping movement with the hand, visualizing the red fire from the inner core of the earth's centre, coming up through the soles of your feet to the heart centre. Then, again with the right hand, pull down the violet energy from the Heavens to the heart centre to combine with the red energy. Do this procedure, three times, and the seven chakras, red, orange, yellow,(the lower three magnetic chakras,)re balance with the three upper, electric chakras, turquoise, indigo and violet, and the heart centre, green and pink is the median.

In this way all the chakras are in correct alignment.

Another method of 'closing down' is to visualize turning off a light switch at each of the chakras in turn, from the crown down to the base. To leave yourself open at the end of a long and busy day, perhaps at an expo, as a reader, is not really safe, as you drive home or cross a crowded street.

If you lead a really busy life perhaps in I.T., you may not have time to pray, meditate, invoke, or talk to your guides, but they will connect with you in your sleep state.

That is when they use symbolism, a powerful medium of transferring knowledge when you are asleep. There can be wonderful vistas, skies full of stars wonderful colours swirling around, so if you are worried that your gifts are atrophying, no, they are being transmuted into a way of connecting with the guides.

The chakras on our bodies correspond with the chakras or power points or vortices on the earth's surface.

First chakra Mount Shasta in US red
Second chakra Lake Titicaca in Peru orange
Third chakra Uluru in Australia yellow
Fourth chakra in Glastonbury, South West of England green
Fifth chakra great pyramids in Egypt turquoise
Sixth chakra in Crete indigo
Seventh chakra Mt Kailas in Himalyas India violet

(In some teachings Crete is the fifth chakra Egypt is the 6th chakra)

There are other important power places on the earth, which are minor chakras.

Also Table Mountain in South Africa is seen as very important.

As the chakras hold very powerful energy, they weave like the caduceus, or figure of eight on our bodies and in similar pattern on the earth's surface.

As seers, clairvoyants, mediums, healers, sensitives, we carry a lot of light. Light bearer is a good name. It does not carry ego for we are carrying it only. And so in our lives we are certain to be challenged by the darkness.

Evil has a scent of decaying matter. We can feel it pervade the atmosphere and here are ways to stop it. You might have thought a certain organization had power, then you saw the abuse of power. Follow your solar plexus and get out! Remember your gut will always give you truth. Call on Archangel Michael to help you. Simple words will do.

Get out into fresh air. Shower frequently, seeing the water taking away any distasteful residue. And work hard, that saves us from too much introspection. Eat regular meals and if u drink alcohol, keep it in bounds for low elementals are attracted to drunkenness and can experience the sensations through our body, the host.

When we are in a heightened state during our work as healers or seers, our aura expands widely several feet outwards from our physical body. If someone should walk through our aura, we feel it as a painful shock, jerking us too quickly from a higher to a lower vibrationary level. Loud sounds have the same effect. Think of touching a spider's web and how it quivers.

Psychic attack is experienced by most of us and it is very unpleasant.

Here is an example. Many years ago my husband and I were invited to a party in Cumbria, in the north of England I took a bouquet of flowers with me for the hostess, my husband took a bottle of wine. The hostess, very attractive and cool looking accepted the flowers and as she did so, they wilted immediately. The room was full of well known celebrities, sports commentators on tv and titled people. There was a frenetic energy in the room of hardly suppressed excitement. I put down my hardly touched glass of wine and said we were leaving. My husband, a keen sportsman, was reluctant to leave but he trusted my gut instinct. The next three days I felt very weak and when I told a good friend, a highly advanced soul, he said,

'Good you left when you did. That was a coven and at midnight you would have seen the occult ceremonies.'

Often when we are drained it can be an unconscious need by someone who is frail or sick, who uses our energy. Sometimes it is a deliberate action.

Very often masseuses get drained by a client, at other times, when there is an exchange, they both feel their energy charged up.

In Mediterranean countries, smudging with olive or bay leaves is used to prevent negativity in the home.

If you are attacked psychically during the night, it might be an odour of evil, or crocodiles' teeth snapping, (very often if it is an Egyptian adept,)sit up in bed and say very loudly."; I STAND IN THE VIOLET FLAME, GET BACK!'

You will see them be absorbed backwards through the planes, as the energy shrinks and withers away.

If the energy is in a house, don't try to clear it yourself, ask a priest or vicar to cleanse it.

Heis qualified to use the sacraments in this way.

A lovely young woman, elfin really, mother of a five year old girl with good gifts as a sensitive came to see me in USA. She was clearing houses but her vibration was high and pure and light. Healing people and seeing for them was a far better fit for her and she became stronger and the little girl happier. in the process.

If you watch tv and the medium takes on the character of let's say the soul trapped in a haunted house, maybe a murderer,. it can't be anything but acting. We cannot go down if we are healers or seers, vibrationally. Nothing adverse can enter into our body without our soul's consent.

In ending this chapter we can look at the terminology of seer, clairvoyant, clairaudient, clairsentient and psychic.

You can be psychic and not spiritual. You can be a bit like a stage entertainer with no spiritual connection.

Spiritual people have a strong personal ethic that characterizes them as apart from psychics, but not all psychics.

Mediums can connect with those who have passed over, people and animals, for they have souls as well.

Seers are born into family groups and see from infancy.

Clairvoyants have vision as their strongest gift.

Clairaudients have hearing as their strongest gift.

Clairsentients feel in their body. Someone might have a crystal ball on their table which is a bridge for them to go into the Inner Planes but they don't see, they feel it in the stomach.

The Romany people who inherit gifts down the bloodline, say that when they left India, way back in time and crossed over deserts where there was no water to scry in, they used crystals like frozen ice. So the crystal ball they traditionally use was a replacement for water.

Chakras spin one way for women and the alternative way for men, therefore the polarity can take place, north and south, opposite south and north. So base chakra red, earth. all about physicality. The one above will spin the opposite way and its colour is orange, water, emotion. The next yellow is fire and it spins in the same direction as the first chakra. And so on The ascending chakras are heart, green and pink, turquoise communication, indigo the third eye centre between the eyebrows and lastly the crown centre, violet. There are additional ones smaller, under the feet, on the nose and above the head, plus others. The chakras resonate with musical notes, the heart being F and also with the minerals which match their specific colour.

Hatha Yoga is a good starting point for the understanding of our soul connection with the body. The physical self is the densest form of spirit. Beyond our physical is the body of light which gets finer and finer as it goes away from the physical. Kirlian photography shows this clearly. The light force which emanates from every leaf, flower and being. can be vividly seen.

Although we have spoken about seers being born that way and people through accidents suddenly finding their gifts, it is a big part, I believe of our work as healers, seers, and spiritual people to bring forward the gifts that may lie latent within a group or an audience. If we demonstrate something, it is not for our own glory, but to show the existence of spiritual connection. When someone realizes that they can'

'See' themselves it's a wonderful thing!

Everyone's powers of intuition can be enhanced with no exceptions. It can open a new world for them and I think it is a large part of our service to mankind to share that knowledge, to raise the vibration of the world.

**2**

The guides connect with us when we are in danger, audibly. Or when there is something vital for us to know, perhaps for someone else's benefit. Guides can be appointed to us because of our spiritual gifts. For example we may be healers and so healing guides will come to assist us. Or we may be seers so those guides who have those strengths will communicate with us. If we were to give up on one of our strengths to concentrate on another, that particular guide will move on to assist someone who needs them. Rather like computers that will analyse our interests from the programmes most viewed. The term guide can be used specifically for those beings, non carnate, (in spirit,) whose job in the Inner Planes is to connect with those of us who are able to make the connection from a carnate (in flesh)place. A diagram to explain this, imagine an equilateral triangle. The apex is the seer, 'standing on tip to' metaphorically speaking, to make a vibrationary connection with an upside down equilateral triangle, the apex of which touches our apex.

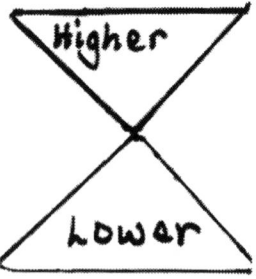

So as we heighten our vibration to make contact, the guides at the other side have to make their vibrations more dense to match the earth plane. That is why mediums, clairvoyants etc get so exhausted because we are changing our physicality to accommodate the vibration of the higher spheres. The water element is essential. It must be topped up continuously, not just a small quantity, like a few sips but a tumblerful between sessions. That is not always practicable if one is working at an expo, but it should be the aim. The area above the kidneys is where the transmutation from liquid to gas takes place. If the energy link runs out of water, and we continue, there is pain in that area.

It is discernible at the end of a day, watching participants looking hale and hearty at the beginning of the event and. at the end, having aged considerably, because of the energy they have put out. The guides at the other side of the apex, presumably, being in spirit will not have an effect as we know it! The Inner Planes and our knowledge from people who have passed over, speak of the many layers in the Inner Planes so an evolutionary process must begin there as well. As we hopefully ascend. Therefore an opportunity of reincarnating to learn the lessons our soul needs for its evolution is hugely important.

We know from the testimony of those who talk about their lives after death is that they work as healers, help others over to cross at the end of their lives who may have died in a similar way to themselves in life and continue to study and learn from the Masters.

Many people have a strong devotion to a particular saint like St Francis of Assisi or St Joan of Arc,. to gods and goddesses like Lord Hanuman (Monkey,) Lord Ganesh, Goddess Lakshmi. The Archangels Michael, Raphael, Gabriel, Uriel, and Metatron are often invoked for help, as are the Virgin Mary, Christ and Mary Magdalen. If there is a strong allegiance to one that we have an affinity with, they also are guiding us in a sense, as we invoke their help, regularly building a spiritual bridge with them.

Our guides may also include a family member who was very close to us and who continues to guide and help us.

Animals who have souls which also progress in the afterlife can appear to us to give us courage. Here is an example.

Driving tests are a terrific strain for most of us who have performance anxiety.

On my seventh test with a huge sergeant major, British, in Krefeld, Germany, I saw Dylan, a badly behaved, much loved, black cat sitting on the back seat of the car. I sailed through the test, knowing my friend was there, caring for me, as always.

Our Guardian angel appointed at birth is our constant companion till our passing. The others can come and go a bit like the Changing of the Guard! As we evolve, so do they.

Another example of the continuation of animals. A good friend of mine, a very talented Seer, was standing at a bus stop in London. A woman was standing in front of her with three spaniels. My friend complimented the woman on her lovely dogs, saying she was an animal lover too. The woman looked at her and said,'I have no dogs with me.':

My friend was annoyed, seeing the dogs clearly in front of her.

"Yes," she said,' you have three King Charles spaniels beside you.'

The woman wept tears of joy as she whispered, They have passed, and what a gift you have given me today.'

One of my favourite sessions ever concerned a very elderly lady in the South West of England. She was very much a country woman, brisk and to the point. As she sat down before me, I said,' There's a horse with its head over your left shoulder. A bay, with an unusual white flash,'

'Oh, that will be Gloria.' she said, matter of fact.

"There are loads of horses behind you, it's amazing."

'Well of course there are, my dear, I'm a horse breeder'.

She was remarkable. She did not want anything about her life, only her beloved horses.

So the guides and I looked at the horses in her herd and told her which she would outlive and which would live on after her passing. From the names we tuned into each, and she mentally worked out where the horses that would live beyond her would go. It was a completely happy session of total unselfishness.

Some months later, her helper wrote to me saying she had passed but how much the session had meant to her peace of mind. The horses were all safe.

I often think of her on Gloria's back, with the other horses streaming behind her. She was inspirational in my life.

# 3

In the previous chapter my friend saw the King Charles spaniels in broad daylight, I saw Dylan in the back seat of a green Bedford vehicle during a morning in Germany.

Another inspirational person in my life was Dave a spiritual worker of exceptional ability, modest, honest and totally truthful in his dealings with people, diplomacy was not in his vocabulary. He told me once of being invited to a Spiritualist church to give a talk.

When he got there, it was a meeting for animals. There were all types there, cats dogs, pigs and horses. As he spoke the whole assembly was totally silent, not a miaow, bark, whimper or neigh. His vibration so very high, that all present would have experienced it.

He was at an expo with other healers or seers.

No one entered the room. Other seers looked over at Dave, saw a man there and they said,' Good for Dave, he's the only one of us working!"

As time went by, they saw that the man was still there. When he had gone they went over to Dave and said,

'That was a long session you had!'

Dave looked up from the book he was reading,

'I've seen no one today.'

When they described the man, how he was dressed in a suit with a bowler hat, he said,

'That would be uncle,' and carried on reading his book.

For his aura to be so powerful that manifestation of that sort in broad daylight and for that amount of time is formidable.

Another example of his gifts was in a roomful of perhaps fifty people, practitioners and many clients and he could observe this incident.

I had gone out for a very quick lunch break, very open, and not having time to close the chakras. In the café in this huge auditorium in Manchester, I was sitting with a cup of hot chocolate for energy, when I saw soldiers marching through the crowd all with kit bags over their shoulders, and all singing.

'It's a long way to Tipperary, it's a long way to go...'.

I finished my drink and walked through the soldiers and the crowd and made my way over to my desk. Dave was over beside me in a moment from the other side of the room.

'What's happened?' he asked.

'There are soldiers, loads of them, marching and singing with kitbags all the way through the crowd out there.'.

A pause then, 'This was a station in the past where the soldiers left for France in the First World War.

That's what you are seeing, then, and now, simultaneously.

Now go and get something proper to eat down you!'

And I did, and the soldiers faded away.

Another truly inspirational person in my life was Mrs. C an elderly woman in Cumbria.

Her gifts, in my view, would have equaled those of the Delphic oracle in Ancient Greece. Born the eldest of six children into a poor family, she won a scholarship being the most intelligent and high achieving pupil in the region.

But poverty and the need to work for her living for her family's sake made her life as a cleaner, an inevitability. So here was this unbelievably talented woman living in a simple house in Carlisle who worked non stop for six days a week from nine am. to five pm. with clients throughout her days. Her clients were cabinet ministers, politicians, wealthy celebrities, poor unemployed and they were treated all in the same way, all equal under spirit.

She would charge only one amount for her services, fifty pence, and she apologized for levying even that tiny fee.

'You see twenty five pence is for my one bar electric fire that I need to have on all day for it's cold in the house, and twenty five pence is to buy a bus for the children of the special needs school round the corner."

No matter how we tried to give her an appropriate amount, she would adamantly refuse.

She bought the bus for the children before her death.

If ever I met an earth angel, it was she, Completely authentic, honest and spent her whole life in the service of Light. I remember once we were discussing Wordsworth's poem 'Ode to Intimations of Immortality' and she refused to accept that there could be a God, I was amazed and said 'How can you doubt it when you have such gifts?'

Her reply was 'I believe there is a healing place
And I hope someplace to find it.'

She could not equate a loving God with the wickedness of the world as she saw it I believe there is a very special place for her where she is in her healing place, helping those who need to be healed, as she lived her life on earth.

When there is anyone self aggrandizing their gifts, I think,' I have known a Master, you cannot compare.'

**4**

There is a lot of discussion between groups as to the difference between being psychic and being a medium. As we said before, being psychic does not necessarily mean being spiritual but surely many are.

Last year I had the pleasure of being in Lilydale in New York state and that was a very interesting experience. Part of my path has been to visit sacred places on the earth so India UK, USA, Egypt, Delphi, Bali, Iona, Findhorn, Rosslyn, and many more which are not so well documented, have given me an enrichening spiritual experience.

Lilydale is in a beautiful area with lakes nearby and rich woodlands, where many seers have lovely Victorian styled properties. It is tranquil and many Spiritualists are drawn there. to do their Light work in a congenial place. Healing temples and the Speaking Stump where mediums deliver channeled messages and the lovely Fairy Wood are some of the places of power. There were debates while there of how Psychism and Spiritualism are very different. Both have their place. Some people will be drawn to psychics and some to seers or mediums.

I was drawn to India from an early age and as soon as it was possible went to visit. When I arrived in Madras, now Chennai, I was overwhelmed by the immensity of the landscape and the hordes of people at the station, really thinking in my hotel room, that I had overestimated my ability to travel round India by train, alone. I had had several offers of companions, but this was really a pilgrimage and I did not want any distractions from meditating in temples or wherever spirit led me. A mass of light gathered on the wall and the face of the elephant god, Lord Ganesh, appeared and said telepathically.

"Do not be afraid! I will carry you around India on my back!"

I totally lost my fear at that point, knowing that the loving protector was with me. He had the most beautiful, compassionate eyes.

After this initial journey I visited the Himalayas many times, having to cope with the military restrictions of Kashmir.

One very holy place, the Golden Temple of Amritsar, a holy place of the Sikh faith fascinated me. Less beautiful than the Taj Mahal but the healing there was tangible. Around the temple, a moat, whose water has the power to heal and every visitor is fed, some porridge type of pudding and raisins Thousands of people visit.

Once in the Himalayas with Rashid the guide, who had seen me in his meditation before I arrived, and who was also a seer, the spiritual vibration was so high in the mountains. I saw eagles, which in Scotland would be a speck in the sky, hover two or three metres above the land. The energy is so high in India, that tears come very easily. There is a heightening spiritually and it takes a few days to adjust.

Egypt has different energy than India. Powerful and mysterious. The presence of the gods in the Valley of Kings, in the temple of Abu Simbel, in the holiness of the Diver Nile itself is almost beyond words.

Near Aswan is Elephant island and there is a temple to the goddesses Hathor and Isis

At Philae, it felt I was walking into a delicate blue mist, stepping from the boat and the presence of the goddesses was very close. Wonderful energy there. Uplifting in every way. If I return to Egypt it is to that area that I would go, to that holy place. I wear an aquamarine pendant in remembrance, from the market stalls selling beautiful minerals and gem stones found in Egypt. Peridots from St John's island, stone of the sun. are a translucent, pale, silvery green.

Travelling in USA I thought I would see Los Angeles. One day to visit the footprints and handprints of the stars was enough! Next day I went to the airport to look for a name I liked, saw Santa Fe and flew in to Albuquerque. There, I was befriended by two sisters who said they would take me to the holiest place in USA, a church rather like Lourdes for its miraculous healing. It is one hour north of Santa Fe which is a really lovely place where musicians and bands play throughout the day. The energy of the area where the church is, is strangely heavy.

Bali is a Hindu island but differs from India in that they wordship the bull, not the cow which is sacred in India because if a woman cannot feed her baby, the cow's milk saves its life. It is an island of many temples and beside one, I had my second meeting with Lord Hanuman, Monkey, much loved god in the east. The legend is that he was the leader of the pack of monkeys and a bush fire came and there was a chasm before them and no way to survive. Lord Hanuman stretched his body across the chasm and made a bridge and the monkeys were saved but Lord Hanuman's back was broken. The gods were so impressed by his unselfish sacrifice, that they made him a demi god, half god half monkey, bit like Hercules in Greek mythology. In this visitation he scampered beside me running ahead then coming back, red loin cloth fluttering in the breeze.

The first meeting was in Simla northern India when I went to visit his temple with nuts in my pocket to feed the troupe of monkeys They surrounded me but again Lord Hanuman stepped forward to protect and the monkeys fell back

Because I have seen two gods in India Lord Ganesh and Lord Hanuman I feel a strong love for both because they helped me on my pilgrimage.

Some years ago I was at an art exhibition talking to an artist, about seeing Monkey. He told me his eleven year old daughter had met him in the woods, in Wales.

Up till that point, I think that I'd believed the Hindu gods would exist in a Hindu culture, but then realised Christ and Mary his mother, both from the Middle East are seen in France USA, Sri Lanka, Cyprus, belonging to the world!

Monkey is a redeemer, Like all the heroes in sci-fi films and Marvel films.

Delphi in Greece was prominently on my list of sacred places, I had loved Greek mythology as a child and as soon as I could read, I pored over my father's history books showing pictures of the pyramids, and I recall the odd feeling when I actually climbed in to the Cheops pyramid, remembering the diagram as a child of four, before I started school.(in Scotland you can begin school at four if your birthday is after August.).

I had expected Delphi to be on a high elevation but it was in a hollow. And made me think of Druidic sites which were always within oak trees and the Greek word for tree dendro always seems to resonate in my mind with Druids and also the word dryad, a nymph inhabiting a tree or wood

The Delphic oracle was called the Pythia after a huge python which was found guarding a sacred spring near or the small township of Delphi. The god Apollo is most associated with Delphi, but he was preceded by the earth goddess Gaia, and her descendants. The Ancients believed he came on the back of a dolphin to Delphi. Apollo is the sun god, and is in his form, as a healer also, Apollo Hylatis. His temple was built there. Legend states that Zeus, the father of the gods, released two eagles from different ends of the earth to find the centre of the earth and when they met at Delphi it became known as the navel of the world.

Kings, Queens, Emperors, Admirals, Generals all came from Greece and further afield in Europe to consult the Delphic oracle, to help with decisions regarding treaties, alliances, and military manoeuvres. Nearby is the sacred grove of Epidabros, sacred to Dionysius, the god of theatre and sacred drama.

Greece is so rich with its wonderful antiquities. Temples abound in the mountains, by the sea, breathtakingly beautiful, architecturally magnificent, with their Doric columns and exquisite proportions. Remembering boring Latin classes at school and then seeing living glory, I am glad that Scotland had this tradition, that all schools should teach Latin and Greek!

Another sacred place in Greece for me was in Crete. Since the age of eleven and reading about the Minoan civilization and temple at Knossos. a few years ago in a very wet February, I flew to Chania from Cyprus and took a local bus to visit Knossos, three hours away.

Only the guide and I were there. The mud that I was trampling through did not diminish my spirits, nor the fact that I was soaked through to the skin, The palace was beautiful the interior decorated in pastel pinks turquoises and gold, of dolphins in the sea., of priests and princes with wonderful peacock feathered headgear. The art, magnificent and joyful somehow. That was my supreme experience in Greece. I left feeling transported with joy and even seeing the soles of my feet, crinkled like frog's skin, being soaked all day long, did not diminish the experience! Was it a spiritual experience? Definitely, for even as I write and describe Knossos, I feel the vibration rise in my spine and I am connecting again with this remarkable civilization. A matriarchal civilization which never experienced a war. From Delphi the statue of the Charioteer stands out most closely.

Like most mediums and sensitives, absolute beauty, in music, in art in dance, in athleticism, in Nature bring us to tears. Perhaps because we see the Divine made manifest.

Greece and India seem very close to me. The first time I was in India I thought it was like Ancient Greece in technicolour, the saris almost identical to the robes of the statues in Greece, the styling of the hair and the jewelry worn by the women. Alexander the Great and his armies would have had a great effect on the population, as they marched ever eastward. The classical beauty of Indian women also echo the proportions of Greek beauty.

I find it fascinating that two people, Carl Jung and Heinrich Schliemann mention in their autobiographies that they knew, from age two, Jung, that he would build a tower that was very important symbolically, and Schliemann had a dream aged four that he would find the treasure of Helen of Troy. Which he did, an amateur archaeologist who followed his dream, Such inspirational men with exceptional spiritual gifts, led by Faith.

Before leaving this chapter, since I have been told by my guides and other seers, that I have to write this book describing all I know, to help others, on the same path, I must include the most exceptional day in the Himalayas. This lockdown worldwide is my opportunity to write!

We set off, Rashid the guide and myself. He, a seer also. At fifteen thousand feet we made camp. This was the pass between the Zanskar and Honza valleys. There were terrorists or freedom fighters holed up for the winter with their rifles on our arrival. Rashid spoke to them calling them his brothers. In the morning we set off early to avoid avalanches that begin at two pm. As we climbed I looked over my shoulder and saw my late father climb to join us, he on my right side, Rashid on my left. We each had snow picks and had to catch each other frequently as we passed over the snow bridge. My father's voice telling me to put my feet at an angle as he'd taught my sister and I when we were children and to" Carry your own weight!"

I saw the rugged mountains and there were faces of kings in the rocks I told Rashid and he said there was a superstition among the people of the region that if you saw the kings you would always be honoured in your life. After the kings a being stepped out from the rock face, smaller than me and I am about five feet two and a half, rather like a goblin in a fairy story. He wasn't attending to us. As we climbed, mushrooms were appearing even as we walked and Rashid said, in the thirty years he had been climbing, man and boy, he had never seen this. Magic mushrooms? I don't know for I feel that if you are born with gifts, there is no need for extra stimulus. Each to his own way. As we climbed to seventeen thousand five hundred feet, our summit, the sun shone gloriously and the clouds formed shapes of angels or fairies in the sky. I found a fossilized shell and my world turned upside down! Had the Himalayas been under the sea? Which had been first, the Valley of Kings of Egypt or the Valley of Kings in India?

There was a presence, we both felt it. An enormous footprint heavily indented at the heel, with four wide toes, and a fifth, falanged at the back, rising in the middle, much wider than the others. I had my camera, but I felt the mountain and the shy being were pure and why would I sully them with taking anything from them?

The highest spiritual essence I have ever experienced was on that day.

The avalanche came just as we got back to camp. We were given so much, spiritually, on that day from the mountains Unforgettable, and my father merged back into the land when we were safely back to base, beyond the river.

**5**

Britain was called The Holy Isles in ancient times. The heart chakra of the world is widely believed to be Glastonbury in the South West of England. As a lover of the tales of the Knights of the Round Table, I was drawn to go there, after reading an article in a magazine, in Brunei, about the sword of Arthur, Excalibur, and the bridge from which local legend said it had been thrown, as King Arthur lay dying.

From the first visit Chalice Well and the gardens touched my heart. The Tor with Saint Michael's church at the summit, majestically protecting the Gardens and the Well, the two in combination, a perfect example of Yin and Yang. The Tor is visible for miles around and I was amazed when a taxi driver, formerly a soldier, told me that he had to live within sight of the Tor, or he felt physically ill. If anyone wants to live there and heal in Glastonbury, they must first live there for a year, to see if they can cope with the vibrations, before they can be practitioners. No matter how experienced they are.

The Gardens are a haven of peace and tranquility. The Well runs reddish because of the iron content of the water, but tradition believed that the Holy Grail, from the Last Supper, was contained within. There is a holy thorn tree which was believed to be the staff of Joseph of Arimathea (a friend to Jesus,) when he visited Glastonbury as a merchant, buying tin. Trading with the Middle East and Greece was commonplace then.

The thorn tree miraculously is in flower in time for Christmas day.

The Vesica Pisces is an interlocked design of circles, making a figure of eight, and it covers the Well. The water flows down two levels At the Lion's head you can drink water from a metal cup there. Or take away the sacred water in a small bottle which you can purchase from Little Michael's cottage at the entrance.

Two years ago, I lead a group to Glastonbury and as we climbed the Tor, I was playing healing chimes for the delight of the sheep at the top, but one black sheep baa 'ed his displeasure!

On that day, as we descended, two of us saw, simultaneously, a huge black raven skimming down to the grassy path with a huge white egg in its beak. We both gasped, neither of us having seen this before, she in Dubai or me anywhere. Black and white. Yin and Yang and the raven, a bird of prophecy and the egg, symbolic of a new cycle or rebirth. I have seen this once more in Cyprus where I live, when a raven flew almost into the windscreen, with an egg in its beak.

Signs and symbols, often from birds behaving in an unusual way have always been read as omens by the ancients from different lands. I see them as heavenly messengers, go~ betweens really. We ask ourselves, how can birds know our situations and communicate with us? Later on, in this book, I will give examples of Nature doing this very thing.

The abbey, dismantled in the time of Henry V!!!, during the Dissolution of the Monasteries contains two very special tombs. The grave of King Arthur and Guinevere, his queen, always has a red rose laid upon it. The tomb of Saint Patrick is also found in the abbey grounds.

Of all the sacred places on earth which I have been lucky enough to visit, the most healing and peaceful I have found to be the Chalice Well Gardens

The whole area of the South West of England is rich, archaeologically. Stonehenge, and Avebury, circles where you can lean against the enormous stones of the latter, perhaps a more loving comforting, maternal energy there, than the mysterious starkness and powerful energy of Stonehenge.

Nearby also. there are the White Horse and the Giant of Cerne Abbas, huge figures cut into the clay, showing starkly bright again the green hillsides, visible for miles around

Women who long for a child traditionally visit the Giant with his huge phallic club in his hand!

Windmill Hill and Wayland's Smithy are also worth visiting. Traditionally if your horse lost a shoe, the elves would shoe the horse for you for a small payment.

The Ridgeway, a prehistoric track includes so many sacred places, a wonderful walk, spanning many days, edging the Downs of Wiltshire.

This whole area of the South is very special, vibrationally on a train from London it is almost possible to actually say at a certain point, the energy shifts here. It is tangible.

Before leaving the South West of England and particularly Glastonbury and its high vibration, this is an incident that occurred during the Winter Solstice with my family.

There were five of us staying in a quaint old inn off the Market Place, at the foot of the High Street, a couple of minutes from the landmark, pre Medieval inn, the George and Pilgrim.

We were having a glass of cider, the local drink, for all the apple orchard owners nearby specialize in their own brew. And apples are seen as magical trees in poetry, legend and literature. A young woman entered the inn and said something to the landlord who told her to leave, which she did, with a few choice words. Next thing, a brick flew through the window smashing glass everywhere. Without a word some old gentlemen got up as one and went out to deal with her and returned to their glasses of cider.

We were taken aback by this wildness in the air, palpable but unspoken by the locals.

Three of our group wanted to climb the Tor. I said, 'It's not safe to do that on the Winter Solstice. It is masculine, wild, energy.'

However they did. Two men, my younger son and son in law and older daughter.

In the morning I was first down to breakfast. My daughter joined me, followed by the men. Her face was bruised down one side and scratched. She said,

'Mum, you wouldn't believe it! I was literally picked up by the wind and tossed down on my face.' Her husband and brother were astounded at what they had seen. The wind had seemed to target my daughter, who was a cross country champion and excellent athlete.

My son in law said,' Let's get back to the safety of London!"' an exnaval diver and explosives guy! So definitely the energy had been hostile to women on that day!

Lesson? Listen to your mother!

The Isle of Man or Mann is roughly equidistant between England, Scotland. Ireland and Wales You can see them all on a clear day. The influence of Scandinavia is very strong on this island Viking traditions, names, beliefs are fascinating and as a seer, the Little People are very close. Even hard headed taxi drivers salute the fairies every time they cross the Fairy Bridge.

There is a waterfall which felt very sacred to me and I felt the presence of the Little People very close. Some might say in that place the veil between worlds is very fine indeed. The folklore of the island would make a lifelong study.

Other areas that I would mention where the veil is very thin, Portland near Weymouth. As I write the word, I smell curry plant and the eyes of the people very often have the same unusual dark rim around the iris which may be green blue or grey and I saw the same in the people of the Himalayas. I wonder where this far back connection was made.

By the Phoenicians perhaps? Mysterious sea faring people.

Robin Hood's Bay, Yorkshire, a vey haunted, picturesque village, built on cliffs.

Burnham on the Sea with phosphorous on the crest of the waves, making it enchanted by moonlight.

Clitheroe in the North of England has wonderfully high spiritual energy. These are the places which resonated most with me as a seer. I am sure there are many more but these are my experiences of sacred England.

**6**

Rosslyn Chapel near Edinburgh with its strong connection with the Free Masons and the Knights Templat which are all interconnected. Scotland has an ancient connection with the Knights returning from the Holy Land after the Crusades were at an end. John Balliol, a short term king of Scotland, endowed the abbey, Sweetheart Abbey in the Borders to commemorate his great love for the Lady Devorgilla. He died during the Second Crusades and she carried his heart in a silver casket which was buried with her in the abbey.

The Knights Templar had an important significance in Scotland, bringing back hidden knowledge of the mysteries. Applegarth in Dumfriesshire is the site of a major branch. And close to Limassol, in Cyprus, there is the castle where Richard Lionheart married Berengaria, at Kolossi castle. In that region the knights had a thriving economy deriving sugar from sugar cane, exporting it widely and. domestically in Cyprus also. The Knights Templar were soldier monks. The Knights of Saint John followed and from that order the Cathars, wearing blue cloaks, believing in Dualism and the equality of men and women. They were mercilessly captured by the Church as heretics and put to the flames.

I n the 'Da Vinci Code,' by Dan Brown, Rosslyn is mentioned as holding the key to the mysteries and in the film, the chapel was used. Its greatest claim to fame is the Apprentice Pillar. A master craftman had to deoart briefly and when he returned he saw a most exquisite pillar. In a jealous fury, knowing his work could never equal that of his apprentice, he killed him on the spot. The chapel had to be reconsecrated but the beauty of the Apprentice Pillar remains.

Iona is a small island of the Inner Hebrides but has an abbey regardless of its size. It is known as the cradle of Christianity in Scotland. St Colomba and a group of monks from Ireland came to Iona and set up a small church, maybe made of wattles, and sent missionaries to the north of Scotland to convert the people to Christianity. In the five hundreds A.D. St Columba wrote that on crossing Loch Ness, he had seen a marvellous beast! The first sighting of the Loch Ness Monster?

The reputation of Iona as a holy island spread from the Seventh Century and pilgrimages were made there. From that time to this.

To get to Iona I flew into Edinburgh and had to take the train from there, arriving early morning in Glasgow. There was a funny encounter at the station. There were only two of us there. A young man, maybe early twenties asked if he could talk to me for he was homesick. I smiled and said,' Of course.' He was Irish and he said I reminded him of Dublin women.

'You talk like James Joyce,

Are you sure you are not Irish?'

I have Irish grandmothers but am Scottish:

'What do you do?' I asked,

'I'm a labourer' he said.

'Well I think you are something else…'

'I am a lawyer but I want so badly to go to Australia and am labouring to get the money for my ticket. I do the two jobs, How did you know I did something else?'

'For you are a literary man, speaking about James Joyce and other poets.'

'Can I come with you please? I hate my work and I have no family here. You remind me of my mother."

';Here comes my train. Now you get into work for ten o'clock sharp and soon you will have enough for Australia!'

'Can I give you a hug?' And we had a close and loving hug!

As I waved goodbye, I was reminded of a poem by T.S. Eliot. That it is not the journey's end that matters, but the journeying.

As the train set off on that remarkably beautiful journey to Oban from Glasgow, with sweeping mountains down to the sea, lochs appearing randomly and I cried when I saw my favourite tree, the rowan, the first time for many years, its scarlet berries glistening in the Autumn sunshine. The colours, pale lilac, misty green, silvery greys that make the brilliant woolllens and tweeds of Scotland so attractive to so many. The land of shepherds.

Oban is an attractive small town built in a crescent round the harbour. In the morning I took a ferry to. Mull, the first of two ferries. I did not like the energy of Mull except for an eagle that flew high above It was grim after the luxuriousness of the landscape travelling up the West coast of Scotland, verdant and rich. All greys and harsh outcrops of rock and no trees The contrast was huge. The bus went from one ferry point to the next for the short four minute second ferry journey from Mull to Iona.

We had sailed as a family, when I was perhaps about twelve, around the Hebrides. I saw the abbey as we sailed past but the ferry boat did not land for the sea was rough.

So I stepped on to the island of Iona with real interest and expectation. A nun had befriended me when we were waiting for the second ferry. I had an uneasy feeling about this black garbed woman, I don't know her faith, her order, or if she just dressed the part with long black skirt and scarf over her head. She asked me so many questions and I asked her none. She insisted that everyone had to go to the abbey that night for some service and I must be there. I found a Bed and Breakfast place which was actually dearer than the hotel at Oban. I showered, got changed and went for a look around. I felt a very old energy on the island, pre Christian, which surprised me after fourteen centuries of monastic occupation of the island. There was only one road which led past the abbey on the left hand side and just beyond, a small cell like structure where one of the saints had prayed in simplicity. That was the one that drew me, not the grandeur of the abbey. In the same way that the Franciscans always pulled me more than the pomp and might of Catholicism, and from the Franciscan simple way, it was an easy step to Buddhism when My seeing showed me that we reincarnate so many times.

So I prayed in the tiny cell hearing the hymns and chanting from the abbey next door, then wandered down to the square near the ferry landing point.

It was very dimly lit but there was a place that served fish and chips and I had a glass of white wine, paid the bill and realised there was no light at all, outside in the square or anywhere, and I had no torch. I knew there was only one road, so all I had to do was walk carefully back the way I had come. I had gym shoes on, not knowing what the island would be like. rough, smooth, rocky or hilly?

Even as I write this I can feel the dread again. In front of me, slightly to the right was a greenish glow. It came from an illuminated map of the island and the nun was there reciting or chanting and to her right an enormous misshapen figure of a man. I went cold with fear. She had tried to get me to go to the abbey for evensong or whatever where every one else was. The light was dim coming from the board. In no way could a shadow have been cast or it would have resembled this small woman.

The chanting or casting of spells and the malevolence in the voice, I will never forget. From somewhere I got the courage to slide past the two beings and quietly as I could, tiptoed past. So engrossed was she, she never noticed. I ran then to the B and B and described what I had seen to my hostess.

She said slowly, 'There are a lot of ancient things before Christianity on this island.

I see things too fairies, elves and such like. I know this woman and she is soon to leave the island.'

She did not take my story lightly and I left the next morning, thinking, I saw the Light and the Dark, together in Iona.

I was relieved to be on the ferries again and spent the night in Oban to restore my sense of normality.

Then on next morning by bus to Fort William and Inverness and then a train to Nairn and on to Findhorn.

Findhorn's story is very well known. In 1957 three people moved to an hotel near Forres. The women were both seers They believed that Nature Spirits wanted them to work on the land to improve it and that this was their spiritual path. So they, all three, worked with the land taking manure to add it to the salty earth to enrich it. An enormous amount of physical work was involved till the site was fertilized correctly. Then they planted, with the help of the Nature Spirits and the vegetables that grew were beyond belief. Scientists and botanists came to disprove but left having to agree that the results were genuine. And the fame spread. Dinner plate sized tomatoes and mushrooms. Cabbages, three times the normal size And simultaneously, a community of spiritual people coming to visit, then wishing to stay. They built ecologically correct homes of all different designs and formed a spiritual community and as it grew the miraculous development in the vegetable kingdom stopped as the seers had been told would happen. First the miraculous growth of vegetables, then the same with people.

When I visited I saw ordinary sized mushrooms, the houses were interesting architecturally, and I was fortunate to be allowed to sit in at a community meeting.

Having been close to communities at various times in my life, Sam ye ling for example, the only Eastern temple in the West founded by Tibetan monks who fled in the 1960's from China, to various places in the world, including Eskdalemuir in Scotland, I saw the same patterns emerge. People used the forum to air grievances. That single parents were not being given help. That too much commercialism was entering a spiritual community and so on. So for me, Findhorn was a disappointment at that time. Perhaps new administration has happened since then. It still has a name to be respected, flower products, oils and tinctures and visiting spiritual teachers come and no doubt in that way, the centre continues to radiate light. The human factor is always the problem with committees and communities, all with good intentions but different dynamics and politics!

My next spiritual visit was in Perthshire, in Aberfoyle, the home of Robert Kirk, the 'Fairy minister.' He was a Presbyterian minister, a seer, educated at Edinburgh University in the Seventeenth Century and he walked between two worlds. He described his visits to the Fairy kingdom and drew them in his diary. Many prominent thinkers, writers and politicians believed him He died aged forty eight years and his body was never found.

His works include 'The Secret Commonwealth of Elves, Fauns and Fairies.' He compiled many legends and folklore of Scotland. What courage he must have had to document how he saw, and his experiences with the Little People.

The energy of Aberfoyle did not disappoint me. Nature and Nature Spirits felt very close.

And before leaving Scotland and thinking of brave men in advance of their time, I recall a book that inspired me when I was around twelve years old.

'The Predictions of the Brahan Seer.' Originally from the Hebrides, born in the sixteen hundreds, he worked as a labourer. He predicted the Battle of Culloden, the Highland Clearances and the discovery of North Sea oil and many other outstanding events.

Always being truthful, he caused huge offence to the Countess when he told her that her husband was being unfaithful, while in France. In a rage she ordered his death and although the Earl on hearing the news and knowing it to be true sailed back and galloped home, to find he was too late to save the life of the Brahan Seer. It is said that the stone he used to see was round with a hole in it and that he threw it into the crowd, saying,

'The man who finds this will be born with two navels. and will inherit my gifts!'

Last century such a man was born.

# 7

Looking now at the way that we see and the different phenomena, the different energies according to the season. and the thinness of the veil between worlds on certain occasions of the year, for example, the Celtic year ended on the thirty first of October, our Hallowe'en, or Holy Evening and the New Year began on November the first.

Christianity took Pagan dates and adapted them into the liturgical year. The Solstices and Equinoxes have different energy again. The full moons affect the tides and our moods!

So if you are a seer, you may well have begun to see in this way. Out of the corner of your eye, you think you see something, then when you turn your head, it has gone and you put it down to your imagination. Because we are realists, right? But the tendency persists and you may see something for a bit longer and you may feel that someone or thing is trying to get your attention. You may begin to notice that you see numbers in an ever repeating manner,1111,2020,4444, 0707 and so on and you realize that when this occurs it maybe close to an important event and. your guides and angels are trying to get in touch, to alert you to something.

Birds tell us also by unusual behaviour or a congregation of birds which is unusual. Owls are sacred to the goddess Pallas Athene, or more commonly Athena, goddess of Wisdom. and doves are sacred to the goddess of Love, Aphrodite. By her bathing place in the Akamas, in Cyprus, the grove is always full of pairs of white doves.

One night a friend and I were travelling to collect archaeological specimens for collating for a museum. I was driving. Out of the ground in front of us emerged a vast white owl, wingspan well over a metre. The huge wings gathered together, surged towards the windscreen, stared at my friend who threw an arm over his face in protection. With a swooping movement towards him, with great power it lifted up and we both continued, shaken, on our way, trying to work out the Visitation, for that's what it was!

'That was the goddess Pallas Athene in her guise as an owl," I said,' and the message was for you'.

We checked for the biggest owl in Cyprus, nothing of that immensity. He had a close connection with Athens, her city, working as an archaeologist. It was hard to keep control of the car, for it was not an insubstantial ghostly owl but powerfully in body as we were.

I often worked seeing the life around the artefact he handed me. The workers who looked like Vikings who wore upper arm ornaments but who were able to work in the Bronze Age period, far away from home, because their gods and goddesses, were the same, different names only! And there was an Amber route in much the same way as the Silk road. Working together with someone who had the professional knowledge was fascinating for both of us. I have joked that I need to be given my dedication at the beginning of a book, film, series, Metaphysical Consultant!

As the higher sight develops we may see orbs, little balls of light, golden speckles, patterns made of right angles showing density and mass. Dimensions seem to alter either expanding or contracting. Time is totally forgotten as we know it as linear time and centrifugal time becomes more of a reality, as you see through the dimensions and people coming towards you from the centre outwards. Light gathers in masses on walls or ceilings and faces appear.

In Singapore I was fascinated at a workshop I was holding. One of those present, completely new to spiritual practice, told us how she was fixing her hair in the mirror and she saw her guide in full manifestation at her right shoulder. She never doubted again, obviously, that spirit is always with us. How lucky she was to have this experience.

And how lucky we were to hear about it!

There is another way that they can communicate with us.

I was at a meeting of the Knights Templar in Limassol. We were seated round a table and throughout the talk, I could hear very soft consistent music, a bit like the humming of a bee. As I looked at a reproduction of a painting of the last Grand Master, his eyes were flickering round the room. At the end I asked the leader what music was playing throughout.' There was none,' was his reply.

In a friend's house in USA she had a Buddha's head in china on the mantelpiece, We both saw the hazel brown eyes in the empty sockets check us out and the room as well. It is now outside as a garden ornament!

When I was in Australia at the large expo there an Italian seer and I chatted at the beginning. He asked me where my gifts came from and I asked him about his.

He said, 'When I was a small child I saw numbers everywhere and I would count everything, the beams in the ceiling, the number of lights in the house. I always knew numbers were holy and I had to work with them. That is how I saw my angels."

We learn all the time and as a great healer, Bobby Running Fox said, 'There is no competition among healers!':

An important difference to understand is that of a ghost and an ensouled being.

A ghost is like a cardboard cut out, an imprint on the ether, perhaps a lot of emotion at the point of death and that imprint remains, discernible to those who are sensitive.

So we might see in an historic house, an image of someone carrying his head under his Arm, like these wonderful Potter stories! We might hear or see both. People often say the air grows very cold before an apparition.

I was in Stratfield Turgis near Basingstoke in an old coaching inn. Every time I got room number eight I would be wakened by a knock at the door, in would come an Eighteenth century rider, crop in hand, who would stride across the room, go out through the window onto his horse, neighing outside, and gallop off. No eye contact just a cardboard cutout, replaying and replaying.

There was also an old man who always sat at the bar then disappeared. Same seat always.

Some places are more susceptible to phenomena than others. Quiet places of historical interest, seem to have their share!

The cat, dogs and horses I referred to in an earlier chapter are not ghosts but are living in a higher sphere when there is a love, protective aspect with those they continue to love giving unconditional love as all animals do. This is a magnetic force.

Sometimes people attract mischievous elves or fairies and they can play tricks, like hiding things, making things move, not like poltergeists which are associated with prepubescent children's energy and their energy is quite violent, pictures smashed and so on. If that occurs a blessing of the house would be the best remedy, by a priest.

Certain plants are good for cleansing like olive leaves or bay leaves burned at the windows and doorways. And garlic or sage.

We lived in a long, low, schoolhouse in the Borders of Scotland in one acre of land with a beautiful old copper beech tree in the garden and primroses on the hillside, when the children were very tiny.

At the foot of the garden there was a stream and it truly was a paradise for the children, skimming stones across the stream and sledging down the hillsides in winter. There was a rowan tree also near the hillside where the primroses grew in spring. Good for climbing. I was teaching at the small village school, the youngest child had a nanny, a shepherdess. The other three children were at school.

We would hear footsteps, always going down stairs, but never returning. The house had been built around eighteen sixty, very elegant in style with pillars by the front elevated door. Family came to visit and they would all tell the same tale, footsteps walking along the passages.

One day, at school, I heard a voice telling me to clean the brass plaque on the wall. I borrowed a ladder and began to climb, with the students looking on, curiously. I read the names, and with Brasso and a cloth, read the names more clearly, John Edgar. leaped out at me, when I heard the voice say,'but they called me Jack!"

Later that week as I took the children for a walk past the church, the voice excitedly called me to look! And there on the War Memorial of the First World War was the same name.

The footsteps steps continued like someone with a limp heavily on one side, but not the other. One night the baby called in great excitement,' Man, man, coat, hat, bees round hat" and taking his hand standing up in the cot he ran his hand down the window pane and licked his finger, again saying 'Man:'

From 9pm every night the energy of the house changed. It felt we were being watched.

Every night I was dreaming of wars and battles and began to keep a diary. They were so vivid. It felt like I was living the life of a soldier in the trenches and mud of Flanders, and by day, I became the village schoolteacher and mother. My husband was taking a group of students to the Lake District for a few days.

I was sitting alone, glad to have some time for myself, reading a Nevil Shute book in the dining room, by the fire when I heard an almighty crash from the girl' room and I waited for the cries of fear. Nothing. I thought, we are being burgled and what can I do? No neighbours around. The phone is in the sitting room, and gathering my courage, I picked up the poker, as my weapon to hit him under the ear.

I heard the footsteps fourteen stairs, threw open the door. The hall was icy cold and the electricity meter was going round so fast and opposite me, at the sitting room door, I knew there was a presence. With every ounce of courage I passed by and and ran up stairs to check the children, All peacefully asleep. I took them into bed beside me for comfort.

The next day I called for a Catholic priest to come and bless the house. I think he was a very advanced soul. These were his words.

'Do not be afraid. This is a beautiful place and may be his Heaven. Reach out with love for love conquers fear.'

Synchronicity at work, no such thing.

Two weeks later an elderly lady in Edinburgh said she wanted to donate her brother's diaries to the village museum and might she please come and visit the schoolhouse where she and her brothers had grown up, her father being the Headmaster.

So she came and we told her the story. When she heard about the baby's description she said, 'When Jack was about ten years old, he and Stuart shared the bedroom your boys are in Bees had built a home in the roof and honey was dripping down the window. He licked it and bees swarmed round his head. He was badly stung.'

She showed us where they buried their beloved dogs on the primrose hillside.

So when the baby saw the man he would have been dressed in his greatcoat and his hat, his uniform. Wherever we went, he came too Aberdeen shire, the Lake District and when I read his poetry, I knew it could have been me writing it. His love of Nature, the foxes, the stream, A medium explained it to me, 'He died at eighteen, never in love and you a sensitive came and he loved you across the Planes. He shared his war with me. My diary dates and his battle dates coincided. I felt the bullets which killed him in my back. The last sight I had of him, was he was sitting on a green grassy hill in his greatcoat waving his 'dishpan' hat in the air, smiling. I never saw him again.

When we visited Yprs and the Menin Gate I couldn't leave the car The thousands of the fallen, golden names, too much to bear.

I often asked myself during this period why I had to experience this, the First World War energy, the proximity of a young soldier, not a ghost, but an ensouled being living in two dimensions at once. If I had had a brother, it would have been him, beyond time, so close.

# 8

Empathy is an enormous part of the life of a seer or healer so that we can help others from the heart. Judgement of others does not exist. We can censure the crime but never the exponent and we are probably unaware of the effect we have as seers, channeling the energy of the guides and their wisdom.

In Shanghai a poor man came to see me. He was at his wits' end. It was a half hour session and he was told in that time, that in a few days, his life would change and that USA would be connecting with him.

'But I know no one there!'

And he left.

Three years later I was in Shanghai and a beautifully dressed man came to see me.

'Do you remember me?' he asked' I have tried to see you so many times but there was never an availability in your schedule.,'

'I was poor then and you told me that in a few days, things would alter. Three days after we met, I got an offer out of the blue to handle all the frozen goods coming in from USA.

Because of the help I was given on that day, the workers I employ are housed, fed, and their children educated. Some are at university and all because of the guides' help!'

We both cried with joy, realizing how spirit works in ever increasing circles!

In Malaysia, in Kuala Lumpur, a total novice came to a workshop I was holding. We were all looking Into our bowls of water, scrying, or trying to. Everyone said what they saw or didn't see and our novice at that point of his spiritual readiness, gave wonderful testimony of what he was seeing. He has now opened his own Healing centre there.

It's a bit like Johnnie Appleseed who walked about America scattering apple seeds as he went!

There are so many instances of women unable to bear children or conceive who are told that they will have children. Often in their forties, when they have given up hope. If I see a papoose on the back, the child comes. It has never failed.

Perhaps I like the story of Johnnie Appleseed so much because he walked far and wide to distribute the seeds.

Sometime times people cry for they don't hear what they wish to hear and they may be Disappointed.

The session always begins with the words 'I work in Light, Love and Truth. Please protect us."

Someone came to see me, year after year, and I dreaded it. She was such a lovely person and so in love with a politician who was married with children. There is no doubt there was real love between them, but marriage, never but there was someone else that I could always see in her future. Six years went by and I thought why doesn't she go and see someone else? Seventh year, she came to see me, brimming with joy.

"You were right! I have met him and we are engaged and my lover told me that he would never have left his family but he will always love me'

I am sure that is true.

When a marriage is dead and defunct they show it to me in two ways. A dead branch from a tree will snap easily over the knee. A living marriage with sap will not break, may bend. Also the analogy of a handful of sand which trickles through the fingers will not sustain growth but a handful of rich loam, will.

Metaphorical language is used throughout sessions with the guides and they often bring up a parallel situation, almost like a memory of another which matches totally the situation at hand. This is visual, like a flashback of a film.

This way of getting information across is very helpful for there isn't really a Metaphysical vocabulary. The transmission of knowledge is beyond words really.

When seers use the word 'almost' a lot, they are not 'covering their backs' but allowing for an acknowledgement of inexactness in using ordinary vocabulary.

So much of our work is non verbal. I was at an expo in UK. As I looked round the room I was aware of a man with outstanding energy. It was tangible across the room We spoke afterwards and I asked him how he used his gifts.

"I am a psychic bouncer." he said. I was intrigued.

"I watch the crowd in the nightclub and when I see an aggressive cloud of red appear, I go over and diffuse it before anything happens.' I was fascinated.

'Actually,' he said,'it is more the women than the men who create the problems!'

# 9

Thinking I should authenticate the title; International Seer;' I applied to become a Consultant of the British Astrological and Psychic Association. There was a strict vetting procedure involving two different examinations for the modalities I had put forward as my gifts. I had chosen Clairvoyance and Mediumship, so four interviews in different localities in London and the outskirts were arranged.

The first interview was with a very talented woman, who said at the end that was Mediumship not Clairvoyance. The second had a great collection of cats so I felt very at ease, they were not allowed to give any indication of approval or disapproval. The third was wonderfully talented with great humility.

She told me after we had finished, over a cup of tea, this wonderful story.

Her son asked to borrow a sum of money to go to a house auction.

She sadly told him if she had it, she would give it to him.

That night she had a dream of the name of a horse, followed by another and a third.

In the morning she told her husband to gather all the money they had, very little, to put on the horse. of her dream. He remonstrated, obviously, knowing how little there was.

When the first horse won, the winnings were put on to the next race, and from then, on to the third race. All three winners.

Almost the exact amount her son had asked for was won in an accumulator. She handed over a cheque to her son who bought the house at the auction, a gift from spirit. She showed me a copy of the cheque. What a great story of Faith! For herself, never.

The fourth interview was easy after the other three. Some weeks elapsed and I was told I had passed with praise from all four.

This gave me confidence to widen my travels to China, Japan, Dubai and so on. I wanted to show a seriousness of intention.

There is another story I love!

A millionaire told me this one. He always placed a weekly bet, as many Chinese like to gamble. He was in London on business and had heard of a very talented Jewess reader.

He was very impressed by her gifts. She gave him, on his asking, lucky numbers.

On the plane, on the way to Singapore he kept going over and over in his mind what she had told him and he could not decide whether to gamble or not.

'She isn't from my culture.'

"She is not a Buddhist like me, she has a different Faith.'

'How could someone of a different Faith and Culture possibly help me choose the numbers?'

And so his decision was made, and for the first time in year, she did not place his bet.

And the numbers were absolutely the same as he had been given.

Had he had enough Faith, as he told me, he would have been a multi-millionaire!

I'm afraid I laughed when he said he had written to her for month's afterwords but it never worked again!

If I am asked for numbers I politely refuse, That's not my scene.

I want to give tools of light to help people to evolve.

I am sure that lady in London was very talented indeed, and she was a teacher for him, really!

# 10

There is a strong connection with Greece in this current lifetime, from the Mythology which was so important to me as a child, in my life in Cyprus where the people have names like Aphrodite, Menelaos, Paris, Antigoni, Desdemona and Iphegenia, the legends still live.

One year with my younger two children we visited Skyros, a very northernly island in the Aegean Sea. I had heard of a holistic centre there and thought it would be good to visit.

We sailed in to the small port of Skiros from Kymi after a three hour journey from Athens by coach. The sea trip by ferry took about two and a half hours.

We found our hotel a few minutes' walk from the port and strolled along the cobbled streets, found a picturesque taverna and ordered a carafe of local wine, a green salad, dips and roast chicken. It was idyllic, looking at the sea and the boats and we were so happy.

Our family room comprised a lower level with two single beds and a short ladder going to a higher level, with a single bed, where my son slept above his head was a skylight.

Our room had a verandah with French windows opening on to it. We were wakened by a wild, highly localized storm It felt as if it were directly over our room. Thunder and lightning and high winds. The French windows were rattling and I got out of bed to fix them.

I opened the doors and there sitting opposite me, in the middle of the night, with no access to our verandah. Except through our room, staring in at me was a beautiful woman with long dark hair. No words were spoken. It was truly sinister. I closed the doors tightly' pulled the net curtains and called up to my son.

'Do not open the skylight window whatever you do.!"

'How did you know I was going to do that?'

'I am praying now to Archangel Michael for protection. There is a woman staring in at us who is sitting outside. Do not look. We are leaving first thing in the morning!' and we did.

Sometime later I heard of the vampires well known in the island who went abroad in the storms and high winds. The old people would never leave their homes after sunset.

In later years I returned as a facilitator at the holistic centre there, and talking to the curator of the museum, he told me of the vampire legends and the many sightings.

This was a totally substantial being not in between planes in any way.

Another amazing experience I had in this area was on a ferry going to Skyros. As I glanced across the ferry boat, a man I had never seen before in this life, was reading a book. I left my body and stood behind him. As the queue lined up to leave the ferry I could see through his eyes and know his thoughts. He was also a facilitator and I told him what I had experienced. He authenticated everything. We worked together a few times and I have the highest regard for his wonderful healing skills and understanding of people. Obviously a past life connection, perhaps of a twin.(.I don't mean a twin flame.)

# 11

I have visited Glastonbury many times and on one occasion a group of family members were invited to dinner in a lovely farmhouse. The owners had spent years restoring it and they had done a wonderfully authentic job. The floors were slate, like grey glass, polished till they shone. On the floors, white woollen rugs, thick and dense like fleece. The walls were left rough stone and the combination of all these natural textures and the huge walk in fireplace, with logs and cones alight, the most striking feature. Were a delight to the senses.

As we sat, enjoying our coffee, I admired the exquisite rugs.

'Would you like the story of this one? she asked.

We bent forward eagerly, for Glastonbury is full of stories.

'My husband and I went away for a short break to London and we asked a close friend to look after the house in our absence.

When we came back, she had left the key and a note to say she hoped we had had a good time. When we came into this room we saw an enormous red stain on that carpet. We were so distressed. All our work and expense spoiled by what? Had she had a party and someone had spilled a bottle of red wine and no one had even tried to clear it up?

We went to the George and Pilgrim knowing she would be there, loving the energy of this 13th Century inn with its oak beams and diamond shaped, stained glass windows.'

She smiled at us,' Oh you're back, did you have a good time?'

We couldn't hold it back and it spilled out.

'What happened to the rug, did you drop a bottle of claret or chianti?'

'Nothing,' she said, looking at us with a hurt expression.

So the three of us walked back to the farmhouse and the rug was immaculate!

She could see how upset we were, accepted our apology and went home.'

'We discussed it at length and deduced that because of the age of the farmhouse that when the monasteries were dissolved, people would have taken the original stone and used it for building the houses in the village or repairing the existing houses. What we had seen was blood, not wine.'

We sat silently, taking this in, goosebumps on everyone's arms.

I was then invited to go upstairs to look at her daughter's room which was experiencing phenomena. The young girl wasn't occupying it at the time luckily. Outside the room it became very cold. Sitting down on the single bed I looked at the pictures on the opposite wall. They were all swaying in perfect synchronicity, backwards and forwards.

'Well,' I said,' I think she should sleep in another room and I'd get the house blessed by a priest, just to be on the safe side.'

We said 'goodbye' and when out of sight, we ran like the wind for our hotel! Laughing hysterically!

# 12

Seers and sensitives use the words, 'through the veil 'very often and they do convey the image very well of density, lesser and greater. For example the vampire described was fully embodied.

A beautiful delicate seeing through the veil happened on a journey driving by the birthplace of Aphrodite near Paphos, a well-known beauty spot, part of a sacred triangle between Amathus, near Limassol, and Heliopolis in Egypt.

As I was driving along, glancing at the deep blue Mediterranean Sea, I realised for the next three kilometers I was driving through a deep violet haze or mist, right across the road. It came from the sea like an aura of heavenly beauty.

Sometimes the veil is perceived clairsentiently and this is what I experienced in India in a hexagonal temple in the South. As I approached the isolated temple which was facing the sea as many temples do, I went inside, after removing my sandals. There was the holy of holies and I wanted respectfully to go in.

It felt like there was a barrier A little like strong elastic, but invisible. I prayed to the god of the temple and asked for permission and the barrier opened for me, to enter and pray.

Another occasion similar to this, was in the rainforest of Borneo. We had a good friend, ban, (sea Dayak) who had invited us many times to the Blessing of the Fields ceremony when the rice goddess was invoked. As Animists, seeing the Divine in fields and crops and animals, and who have family totems like their cousins in North America, (Which may be monkeys, lizards, turtles and crocodiles,) they blessed the planting of the new crops with sacrifice. I didn't know this and at a certain ceremony, I was chatting to a young Iban who was at University in Australia studying Ecology. A keen football player.

The Shaman with his long silver hair tied back and his feathers in his hair, his staff in his hand, drank the traditional tuak, rice wine, and the gonalong soft drums kept the beat. The young student went into the chest of drawers of the longhouse and drew out long slim sword. He had a white cockerel under one arm and as I glanced across to the other side of the hall, common area to all of the families who had their own homes under the long roof, I realised they were going to sacrifice the cockerels!

The thoughts that flashed through my head…. I can just grab the cockerel and run!

But won't this be a terrible insult to the tribe and their culture and might there be a bad harvest as a result?

So I left the longhouse, got into my jeep and began to drive slowly and quietly away.

It was almost impossible to drive. The energy was so strong and it felt like hands were reaching out to hold me back from leaving. That same kind of invisible elastic grid stretching across the track. The further away I drove, the easier it was to drive.

The years in South East Asia were extremely interesting. On another occasion, three of us were in the jeep. We were going through a border crossing from Sarawak to Brunei and I took a wrong turn. Almost immediately, there was no light, the jungle was all around and as I was feeling uneasy as the driver, each of us said, simultaneously, 'Think we should go back, there's a strange feeling about this place.'

So, doing a five point turn, we drove back to the crossing.

I think it should have been a three point turn but I did not want to end up in the deep ditches, cut to drain away the heavy Monsoon rainfall.

We all began to talk again when we were safely back on well-lit roads.

'What was that all about? Felt like we weren't meant to leave.'

That some force was trying to keep us from leaving.

All felt exactly the same energy.

I was told by locals afterwards that this was the area where the Bomos met to work.

Medicine men? at best, Perhaps spell makers at worst!

With a large group of people we watched my Iban friend do the Hornbill Dance, a sacred dance with coins around the dress. Gonalong music accompanied the dance. When the lights failed. We watched entranced, as the beautiful magical dance continued with lighters held up to provide light. An experience we will never forget. Total silence!

My friend was leaving to go to university in Brisbane and there was to be a blessing ceremony to wish her well. We sat in a circle, her family and friends, and the Shaman was present to do the ceremonial aspect. The bard of the tribe was sitting next to me, a woman of prestige, who would heal and sing the dying into the next world.

On the mats were the foods with the sacred numbers, three, seven and nine. Three fish, seven cakes and nine eggs. The cakes and eggs all painted in different colours.

The Shaman broke a raw egg to each of the directions, North, South, East and West

My friend stood and behind her I could see Hercules a strong powerful being with upper arm ornamentation, a kind of kilt and behind him a female being with a skirt to the knees, again with a belt of coins. I felt she was connected with the arts and wisdom.

I whispered to the bard,' Look at Hercules and the lady with coins!'

She looked at me sharply and said, 'You can't see them, you are not Iban!'

We learned a lot from each other from that day. That if you are a seer you will see, but you might put a different interpretation on it if you are from a different culture.

I identified that powerful being as Hercules.

Interestingly, a writer of the Iban myths, himself Iban, compared their theocracy with that of Ancient Greece in Greek mythology.

Which begs the question, are they the same gods and goddesses which were told, (there is no written language,) by bards who tapped into universal consciousness or did explorers carry the tales? An artist friend once said the same thing about similar art movements springing up sporadically all over the world, when there was no physical communication.

Later we will find out about the Black Moonstone of Borneo which captured my imagination for years!

# 13

I was walking along with my late husband and younger son in the grounds of Marlborough College in the South of England.

I heard a voice calling me loudly, 'Come to me!' It was a commanding voice!

I began to run towards the Motte, (meeting place,) a conical, treeless hill which was to my left.

My husband asked me what I was doing, but I was running too fast to reply. And it seemed an irrelevance to reply, really.

I began to climb the hill.

About a third of the way up, a man appeared to me, on my left, as I looked ahead. He was wearing a long robe with a cord round his waist, bearded.

He spoke to me and said,' You are a healer. I will teach you.'

He turned and pointed to a deepwater font and said "Look within, when you need my help.'

He pointed to the small square headed bird sitting on his shoulder.

He had the kindest warm brown eyes and I was transfixed by his words and presence.

He disappeared and I went back down the hill.

I was met with anger. They had searched for me for an hour and a half with no sign of where I had gone. I felt I had been away for three minutes.

There were no trees, rocks or caves, just a smooth green hill or Motte.

The small square headed bird was a merlin.

Legends say he is trapped inside a hill waiting for the day when England needs him.

The word' Marlborough' is derived from Merlin's borough which I later discovered.

I believe I went through a portal for there is no way I could have disappeared otherwise.

And now I can understand why it would have been so frightening for my husband!.

Portals are not fixed, they move. Like the best experiences, they seem more profound when they are unexpected, say you are discussing a film you watched, or singing to yourself when you are driving.

As I look back on Easter Sunday, I realize that he dressed a bit like Saint Francis of Assisi in a rough woolen gown. It was a miraculous appearance and experience in my life as a seer.

There was a portal in a friend's house in spring field. MA. There was the front door and superimposed upon it in light another doorway. We could hear voices and movement at the edge of sound.

In North America I had another incredible experience, this time in New York state.

I had travelled from Albany to the friend's house in which I always stayed. I had just unpacked. It was late on the fourth of July, Independence Day, around midnight. The beautiful wooden house stands back from a large pool or a small lake and there is a duck house on the verge. It is a large property and feels sacred somehow. Native American influence around is the energy.

A light caught my eye. I thought that must be my friend with a torch making sure the ducks were safe. Coyotes and foxes are there. Then I saw, popping up from the ground all around, lights like lanterns a few feet above the ground, perhaps thirty in all, weaving about like children getting into a rough column at school. They glided along the side of the lake as I watched, mesmerized. Finally they disappeared into woodland still on her land. The lights approximated in size to the head of a large torch.

I explained at breakfast what I had seen and walked their route. She told me there was an underground stream which the path they had taken followed.

Looking at possible explanations, Fireflies, way too small.

Marsh gases way too organized and they don't have that in the environment.

Lit paper lanterns drifting on the wind.

None fitted, then a year or so later, met a healer in the South of England., well known to Me, with great gifts.

He has been a biker, Merchant Navy guy, covered in tattoos who has the ability to talk to fairies. I described what I'd seen in New York state and he said,

'Easy! You saw the Nature Spirits out doing a bit of cleaning1"

It felt so right and I thought isn't it great that they are keepers of the environment!

That same man told me of his experience looking at two fields, wondering which to buy.

He heard fairies in the hedge talking and said to them, 'You're being a bit noisy, aren't you?.'

They stopped, looked at him and said, 'Can you hear us?'

"Yes,' he replied, 'what should I do with this field?'

'Something nice,' they replied and disappeared.

On that same property in US, I saw rainbows in the snow, the title of a book I wrote, and on another occasion when my friend and I were sitting on a bench looking at the lake, a silvery large object came up and shot towards us at a great speed. It disappeared at the bank. We both saw it vividly. The surface of the lake was dark. No phosphorous like the sea near the West coast of England, Burnham on Sea. Impossible that a fish could either swim at such a speed or in a dead straight line. I thought about electric eels, but they are not native there.

In the examples in this chapter there has been no prelude of meditation or prayer or talking about supernatural things, just ordinary living!

The questions would seem to be these. Do we interact with the area as sensitives and cause a reaction in the earth? Is it happenstance that we happen to see and experience these things? Are they part of the normal life of seers? Are they trying to teach us, to get our attention, or part of our spiritual path?

This tale, told by two women whom I know and can vouch for their integrity, occurred on a drive to Temple Combs. They were going to have afternoon tea, cones with cream and strawberry jam in a favourite hotel.

As they drove through, one remarked, 'I don't remember seeing this church before and the other looked and agreed that she hadn't seen it either.'

Some hours later, after an enjoyable afternoon tea, they drove back through the same village, but this time the church wasn't there.

They went to the library and asked the librarian about a church.

'Yes,' she said, 'there used to be one where you describe it but it burned down in the Seventeenth Century.'

Were the women both sensitives? Were they entering the Seventeenth Century for a moment? Did a portal open up beyond time and space, allowing them a glimpse, or is it that we live in parallel realities?

Or was it a time when the veil was thin and the date, that they travelled coincided with the place, and their own gifts, and the three points of reference came together?

It reminds me very strongly of the German class at school, reading the story by Goethe called' Germels'Hausen'. In that tale the village came back every hundred years for a day.

# 14

In Australia, I dream all the time. As soon as I fly in, the dreaming starts that night. This never happens in any other country. The Aboriginal culture speaks about the Dream Time and probably their belief system has for so many thousands of years impacted on the psyche of the land. Or, it could be the other way round, that the Aboriginies tapped into what was already there, that in this place on earth there is very little differentiation between the planes. For me Australia is the Land of Birds, their calls and songs and behaviour so different from any other I have known.

The population is so small and the land mass so great, perhaps it has kept its purity.

I was flying from Melbourne to Brisbane, a short journey. As I was looking out of the window at the sky, a face appeared right in front of me in the cabin. An Aboriginal man looking at me very keenly as if assessing to see if I were worthy. Then he disappeared. I had never had any visions on planes and I fly frequently to different continents.

I felt honoured that this spirit of Australia had visited.

There are three categories that I see. One is a dream which lingers, perhaps for a few hours and disappears.

The second is a vision and that never leaves you. It is part of your very being. Carl Jung puts it very well in his autobiography, and I am paraphrasing here, 'meeting kings, queens and dignitaries were never as important to me as the visions I experienced from an early age. They were the signposts I followed.

And the tower, he first encountered as a tiny child, he built in middle age, physically on an island.

The third, when an angel may appear before you, a saint, a god or goddess figure, your shamanic animal. Which is not from within your psyche but out with, coming to the meeting place as it were.

The visions you have, the second category are meaningful and give your life direction, I believe. And the third category are spontaneous when our spiritual journey warrants them

We may experience déjà vu when we connect with a place known to us from a previous life time. It feels familiar and we know what lies round a corner. Our soul is recalling past life time experiences.

While' rings pass- not' are put in place between life times, so we don't get overwhelmed by the experiences of more than one life time, the soul carries traces of certain characteristics that have been a constant throughout. In my case and it has been verified, I can't break a promise. It makes me feel physically ill if I am stopped by matters beyond my control, like a plane is grounded.

If people like us, seers, sensitives can consult the Akashic Records where everything is recorded, then our thoughts are indeed things and become manifest into action and deeds.

Simultaneous time? Parallel time? Synchronicity? Coincidence? all showing Divine timing way beyond our limiting Linear time which, of course, is an illusion.

Emotional time, influenced by our feelings, happy, sad or frightened. They are not fixed.

Now as the world is closed down and our freedoms limited for the good of the many, a week has a totally different meaning as we have the opportunity to go inwardly, reflecting.

We may be so busy in our day to day lives that there is no time for going inwardly, it is enough to do the day's work with travel, home, shower, eat, play with the children and sleep. Our guides will teach us as we sleep. Those who have lives like this have shared with me the incredible colours and vistas of stars like countless diamonds in the sky with virtually no space for dark night sky between. Of gods who come to comfort, of lying in the hand of God.

# 15

Near death experiences occur in many lives and nothing is really the same afterwards for our lives are seen from a different standpoint.

I had always wanted to give birth to my children at home and in fact had my sons in hospital and my daughters at home.

After a miscarriage. I was again pregnant and kept teaching, one day a week only and felt the labour pains come when in class which was a bit worrying. However like many mediums, our children are born after a long labour. Quickest was a day and a half and the longest four days. The night nurses would say, you are not still here! And the book which kept me absolutely sane in that period was. '.the 'Beastly Beatitudes of Balthasar B' by J.P. Donleavy. Hilariously, wickedly, funny book!

My time came and the baby girl was born, but there were complications. A twin which had never been noticed in the medical checkups was delaying the afterbirth and I was losing a great deal of blood, hemorrhaging. There was so much confusion but I knew when all the colours faded into black and white and I was going through a tunnel that I was leaving and I remember clearly saying to myself, 'Imagine dying in childbirth in the Twentieth Century!'

As I came through the tunnel into the light, there was an ocean of love and, imagine the happiest day of your life as a child, and multiply that by a hundred or a thousand times.

A voice said to me 'You have to go back.'

I said, 'No, I like it here.'

And the voice said, 'You must go back. The children need you.'

After that I was very weak for six months unable to do the lightest dusting even.

The contrast between the ocean of love and the scratchiness of the earth plane and its problems, I can still recall so clearly.

From that time, I have never feared death, knowing what's on the other side of this reality. The other twin had not grown, so I feel I am the mother of four children, with two in spirit. So what we do with our lives matters after that experience, to live each day to the full, bringing our gifts and strengths forward, in whatever way we can.

# 16

Skyros, the island where we had our nocturnal visitor, and fled from the island on the first ferry, was described by Homer as the Windy Isle and certainly every time I visited thereafter, the wind was always blowing. The months I visited were July or August. The streets are narrow, twisting and cobbled and the interior of the houses, beamed, and quaint. Carving of wood in the interior was am attractive aspect.

An interesting feature in the sitting room, about two thirds of the way up the wall there are shelves displaying plates from all over the world Whenever anyone would get a new plate, it would be a matter of celebrating, inviting the relatives, friends and neighbours to inspect the latest addition! The geographical position of the island, close to the mainland of Turkey, meant a lot of influences would impact the island's culture.

It amused me a lot to think how similar we all are. In the west big cars and houses, or in the past, a piano in the parlour to impress guests and in Skyros the best collection of plates! Always a way of striving to be better!

There was a Spring festival in Skyros that sounded very interesting, held in February and people who had emigrated, came back in droves, from USA and mainland Greece, Germany, from all parts, for this ancient festival.

Living in Cyprus and knowing how bitterly cold winters can be there, I flew to Skyros well prepared for an island much further north, in February. Thick winter jacket, warm woolens, bed socks, the lot. Some people, only a small group, had turned up with summer clothes, sunscreen oil and sunglasses. The last were actually needed if the sun shone in the bright Hellenic skies.

We had stayed in a hotel in Athens as the group gathered, and travelled up by bus to Evia.

The weather was wild. Being a really bad sailor I went to buy sea sickness tablets from the chemist. The others laughed saying, 'I never get sea sick.' That was the consensus of the group. so I just smiled and took the ribbing!

We got on the last ferry. The captain had been in two minds, for it was a Force 8 gale. I had taken two tablets and the boat heaved and swayed in the darkness, huge waves and winds, battering the ferry boat, as we huddled in the large lounge. The braver souls went up on deck to look at the sad souls who were stranded on Evia, knowing there was no way they could make their annual pilgrimage to their homeland. It was to be a whole weekend of ceremonies.

One by one, the faces of the group turned green and the leader of the group came and asked me if I would share the sea sickness pills with the others, which I was happy to do, with no trace of smugness! The crossing took three hours and we were glad to get off the ship. The captain was a hero, really.

We were fortunate to have an invitation next morning to watch the Yeros, one of the men, chosen by the church, for the honour of leading the ceremonies, prepare his costume.

This was, and is, a Rite of Spring, predating Christianity, and well over two thousand Years old, an unbroken tradition. Although Pagan, the Greek Orthodox church gave the ceremony its blessing and choose the men most suited for the roles they play, If I say it was a privilege to watch this ancient rite, it would be a huge understatement.

We were taken to the room where the man was putting on the white woollen base. First a long sleeved white woollen garment and the same for the long johns, very thick and very warm. The socks, white and handknitted. Every garment had its role to play rather like a priest robbing for Mass. Then a thick hump shaped pad was placed on the back and strapped on tightly. On top of this was the skin of the goat. Around the waist a thick leather belt from which hung many copper bells. The sandals were also made of soft animal skin.

The atmosphere in the room was changing. As soon as the skin of the animal was placed over the hump, the man became the spirit of the goat. Lastly a white mask from the skin of a young goat, was placed over the face with only eye holes visible. Finally a shepherd's crook was placed in his hand decorated with a small bunch of spring flowers.

In all, the weight of the costume was fourteen kilograms, so very important that the belt and fastenings were strongly in place, for often, men had suffered serious back injuries in the ceremonies. Once the dressing stage was over, with a leap and a bound the yeros took off into the narrow streets, glistening with rain, as the rain had never stopped since our arrival.

It was so cold! and as all the people on the island lined the streets, the yeros,'old men' were bounding and leaping in no order, some in one street, some in another, but never together till they met at a crossroads, then, with a mighty leap, they all jumped high into the air, waving their crooks dramatically. And the running continued for hours, the bells around their waist, ringing, loud and primitive. The cacophony lasted till sunset.

The following morning, it began again, as the running men danced and leaped in the air

And it really felt the island itself was participating in a Pagan outpouring of joy and release and passion. And everyone was affected, the old and the young, and still the bells rang loud and clear, almost hurting the ears. People ate and drank in the tavernas, happily chatting to the family members who had returned and made it to the island.

Although they were yeros, 'old men,' this really meant 'ancient men,' for the weight they were carrying, and the sheer physical endurance needed, could only be performed by strong men.

On the stroke of midnight, on the last day, the bells stopped simultaneously. And Miraculously, it seemed, the rain stopped exactly at the same time.

In the morning, the sky was a clear, cerulean blue and the sea was calm as a millpond

And the silence was shattering!

When we think of Bacchanalian rites of freedom, wine, intoxication and revelry that must be close!

Women were also involved in the ceremonies, wearing Greek national dress and waving a handkerchief as they danced along in front of the Yeros.

I have watched mediums in a Chinese temple raising the power through drumbeats and being able to walk on hot coals and pierce their skin with swords, but this never moved me as much as the Rite of Spring in Greece.

The response of the earth itself was so moving.

And the collective energy, of all of us present, would have built in the Planes of Light also.

# 17

The people I have met who are seers or clairvoyants, mediums, healers, all water by another name, have often given up their professional careers or businesses, for they feel the pull too much, not to give up the material, for the spiritual.

One such, gave up his life as a millionaire businessman to be a psychic surgeon.

Now I had read about this, along with leylines, power places on the earth's surface, potions of South America and so forth, as we all investigate and learn when we are seekers of the truth. It is an important part of our progress, though we finally accept that we learn most, by going inwardly and experiencing for ourselves.

I had an opportunity to observe a psychic surgeon at work in UK and I made sure that nothing would escape my eagle eye and I took my position right at the front, perhaps three feet back from the patient and the surgeon.

The ailment was the shoulder which could not move and had been a problem for years. The surgeon had no long sleeves where he could conceal anything that I'd read of, like phials of blood! There were maybe twenty people in the room. Many of these were fellow healers and mediums. The surgeon placed his hands on the patient's shoulder, the higher gifts kicked in, and I saw a speeding up of energy, whirling around the shoulder joint, like a vortex, and this was in black and white. I saw the arm remove from the shoulder socket like a doll's arm, and then, in an equally fast vibration, the arm and the shoulder recombined.

The patient sat up, crying. The pain had gone and for the first time in years he could raise his arm freely. They were tears of joy and also probably because he felt the high spiritual vibration which can often make us cry, trying to adapt from one level, to another, too quickly.

After the demonstration I sought out the people I knew who had really good gifts and asked what they had seen. One said, like me, black and white, very high vibration, the next saw in colour but the same thing and the last saw in colour but also saw a knife in the hand of the surgeon and he saw blood. We all were convinced of the complete movement the patient now exhibited. I have since heard that the after effects of psychic surgery don't last but I can only speak about what the others and I witnessed.

**18**

If we are born with the gifts of seeing, healing is there as well. I wanted to be a healer and studied so many modalities. Reiki Master level, Neuro Linguistic Programming, Yoga Hatha and Rajah, Colour and Crystal Healing, Sound healing, Flower Essence Healing (USA one and a half years,) Ayurvedic medicine for minor ailments, massage and oils, for years in Brunei, and spiritual healing in UK.

However everyone wants the seer. The guides told me some years ago in USA that I was to give three relevant past lives in each session which I now include, and also later, to make my own cards with the guides, using Encaustic wax, for like water, wax is an excellent conductor. At the end of every session which is purely oral, the cards are chosen by the client and invariably, they authenticate the truth of the session. If they are told marriage in the session, they will choose the marriage card. It has never been wrong in all these years.

As a seer I like to teach also, and I feel it is an important part to proceed now with some teaching strategies for bringing forward gifts, either for yourself or for others.

I also emphasize, in workshops or lectures, how important it is, to stress that there is no right or wrong way, it is as each individual perceives. So although I may be leading the discussion, the newcomer to the group can have remarkable gifts which is a wonderful thing to see! The gifts we have may be demonstrated for a short time, always with the words, 'You have the same gifts of intuition so let's bring them out. Building the confidence in a safe, non-threatening, cooperative, compassionate, environment is essential.

It was with a group in Singapore when we tried this experiment. I explained I had never tried this before with people who were there as total novices and I didn't know if it would work.

We dimmed the lights a bit. I sealed the room in the relevant way, by prayer by Reiki symbols and most importantly, by intention.

Someone sat in a chair and closed her eyes. We focused our eyes on her and soon saw her eyes, physical ones closed, be superimposed by eyes which were open and a different face appeared. It was fascinating to watch as each person in the room took a turn of sitting in the chair and also being an observer. Everyone experienced both states.

At the end of this session we closed the energy of the room with a prayer and everyone was happy and aware that we all, equally, had this ability. And spirit presence was proved absolutely.

Very occasionally someone can transform, and speak, simultaneously.

It is good to do something you haven't done before in a workshop. You are testing yourself and I believe the guides never let us down.

Before any session I begin with the words, I work in Light, Love and Truth as I have said

Previously, and nothing untoward can harm us.

One way of bringing on the gifts of others, is to tell them to bring, or practice at home with a clear bowl, glass or plastic, and half fill it with water. As they sit on a chair or cross-legged on the floor, they look into the water, silently, for a few minutes. They will notice the breathing deepening and the eyelids becoming soft as they relax, looking into the water. They might see nothing, or something quickly out of the corner of their eye, or something more. This is something they can use at home for relaxation after a busy day at the office. It transports everyone into a heightened mental/spiritual space.

Another way to teach a group to be more sensitive is to encourage them to find a short time in the day, when they will not be disturbed and make that chair, that space of time, a regular feature of their day. Let them work out which category of person they are, visual, auditory, or sentient and let them mentally ask their guides to give proof of their presence. There might be nothing at first, then perhaps a whisper, or the lyric of a song, or a feather light touch on the cheek, or the scent of a flower.

Very soon, this practice will be incorporated into the day when there is time for a spiritual vibration to become a part of the daily life.

Visualization is also an important tool for heightening our spiritual vibration, as well as prayer, invocation and meditation. Visualizing a memory of a beautiful place or event in one's life and feeling truly in that energy, makes even a journey by train or tram a much more pleasant experience. Training the mind to be aware is important. Are we repeatedly going over old ground, old grievances, instead of living in the moment with happy thoughts, which we choose to bring to mind, choosing positivity instead of negativity.

We are mostly challenged in the carnate form at the emotional plane level. That's what it means to be human, to feel. We suffer loss, fear, despair, and scarcity, hopelessness at some point in our life, as well as joy, happiness, optimism, excitement, passion, and exhilaration. We can consciously stop ourselves veering towards the first category by being mindful and observant. Our thoughts are things and can bring into manifestation what they focus upon. A cheerful outlook and demeanour attract the same kind of people and good things. The reverse is also true.

Events also shape our spiritual development. When there are challenges, do we reach out to others in their time of need or are we too self preoccupied?

# 19

As seers, we all have different gifts and talents and have different ways of working. Some might be pulled to platform demonstrations, others to group work, others to individual sessions, others to developmental work through classes or workshops or lectures. Mostly we do a mixture of all of these, healing simultaneously. So our body of work includes a wide variety of ways of reaching out to others, raising the vibration of the Universe, for these gifts are for that purpose.

Because everything in the Universe vibrates, even the chair we are sitting on, minerals have a real place in our lives. We are pulled to them, often not realizing why, and they are helpers! When we think about watches and the use of quartz for drills we realize how much the world depends on them, in industry and so on.

I have a rugged piece of green calcite which travels the world with me. Since the clients are from all cultures, it would be inappropriate to have any specific religious symbol on the desk but minerals are different.

This specific mineral called to me as I was walking, exhaustedly, though a crowd at an expo in London. I didn't know if I could make it to the end of the day. Stall holders had been giving me goji juice as I walked along so I must have looked really spent, doing four fifteen minute sessions in an hour and it was close to the end of the day.

As I walked by a mineral stall my name was called. I looked at the minerals and the green calcite said, 'Take me home with you.'

From that time it goes everywhere. I had heard the voice telepathically. It had felt my need and had responded. I notice children are always drawn to that mineral though I have others also and they want to touch it. Some people won't allow that but I like it, for all minerals except one, zeolight, are emanating, giving out to the Universe unconditionally. Also this green mineral belongs to the heart chakra which is green. Colours are important and correspond to the main chakras on the body and on the body of the earth. Correspondences of colour, crystals and musical notes.

As a small child in Scotland, my sister and I would walk near a loch and look for minerals like jasper, amethyst, cairngorm and agate. I loved the patterns on agates and still do, the banded ones and the moss agates are particular favourites. Little pictures inside. When our grandfather took a hammer to the round pebbles, found the fault line and we saw the geode inside, in all its crystalline glory, we were thrilled!

Minerals have been a huge part of my life as a seer. Holding them in my hand when afraid, that was an occasion when I was going to give a clairvoyant or mediumistic message to fifty advanced psychics and healers. I don't like any one to be omitted from a demonstration and so always give everyone a message where practicable. The mineral I held then was a smoky quartz crystal and it was an instinctive choice. When I checked up about it later, I found they were carried by First World War soldiers into battle. The session went well and everyone received a message except one. I felt he did not want me to do this and asked him if this was true and he said, 'yes.' It is important to ask if people want a message or to indicate with a shake of the head that they don't.

As a very small child I saw a beautiful piece of glass with inclusions of white speckles. It looked like frozen water. I now have something similar, a very delicate watery green Andara mineral, natural glass, another exquisite turquoise Andara, gifted to me in Singapore which I love, and a clear glass mountain shape with rainbows inside which I thought was quartz but an expert told me another Andara. They have very high energy.

My mineral collection mostly sit outside to get sun and moon and starlight. It saddened me to see dust collect on amethyst clusters in mineral shops. A friend, crystal healer, told me she uses a feather duster and that she can almost see them wriggle with pleasure like having a shower! Mine are shining in the sun as I look at them outside, close to Nature.

To revitalize them, wash in clear or sea water, leave them in the sun and a Full moon if you can, to rebalance and top up their energy. It is not always possible to do what I do, I know, but you might have a window box or a big plant that would like to have a mineral companion?

The Black Moonstone of Borneo which I mentioned before is a very important part of my life.

When I arrived on the island of Borneo, on that section which is the country of Brunei, I heard about the Black Moonstone of Borneo. It felt like a magical spell was laid on me. It fired the imagination, whereas a diamond would have had no effect at all, run of the mill stuff, a black moonstone, what could it look like? A contradiction in terms!

So people told me, you will never find one. You might look for a hundred years and never find one. But I had Faith.

Some months went be and I was in an old Chinese junk shop. It had china, paper lanterns and a dusty velvet display case with inexpensive minerals set in bronze or an alloy like that. Second row back, I thought I could see one My heart was beating so fast I could hardly get the words out.

'Could I see that one please?' pointing to it. Trying to look casual, I held it in my hand and I could feel its heart beating. I bought it. Delirious with joy, my life's ambition and there it was!

Younger son was staying with me. I told him in great excitement that I had found a black moonstone of Borneo against everyone's predictions.
'

He put out his hand and he said, 'I feel a pulse beating.'

I knew what I was being asked by the guides.' If u feel that, it's meant for you.'

He said,' No way, I know what it means to you.'

In the end we decided to toss for it. He refused to call. I called and it was for him.

'Best of three,' he suggested, (but that's not sporting) Then half a year each. Then lets' cut it in half. The jewelers shook their head. So deciding on a silver setting, we went back to the little shop and left the mineral for a few days. When we went to collect the ring, they were evasive and eventually the man said 'That stone is exceptional and my brother doesn't want to part with it.'

Because I had already paid for the setting, he phoned his brother who came reluctantly to pass it over. My son, back in London was telling his skeptical friends about the stone, and they were scoffing and falling about. The Grand National, the biggest race in Britain was on that day, so my son took his last five pound note and put it on a horse, a rank outsider. Which. came in first, at odds of twenty seven to one and his friends were no longer laughing. In fact, one borrowed the ring for an interview at which he gained the position.

The hunt was on again. An elderly French woman who knew the significance of the stone from Chinese soldiers, her late husband had been in the army, so she chipped a few bits off hers. And gave them to me.

Again I was over the moon and again thought, is it for me? We took the pieces to a Chinese car mechanic whose blowtorch was strong enough to weld the pieces together and at a goldsmith's, we found a golden cage in which to place it.

Again it felt it was not for me, but my daughter.

After that, giving away the second time, they flowed to me. I found them in streams.

As soon as I gave them away to family and friends, more would flow in. It was really strange I found one so big, like a curling stone that it had to go to the Royal family who, as in Malaysia, have the right to these minerals. I found over a hundred, not even looking for them. I might walk into a shop and say, "Can I see what's in that dish up there on the shelf?" and yes! There would be a collection of beads. It was truly miraculous!

I am wearing a simple gold ring with one of the beads set in it the gold setting made by a goldsmith at his small wooden table. (My son told me to give one of the moonstones to the brother who had sensed the exceptional properties of the stone, and I did.)

The lesson for me was, when you give up what you value most, the Universe will give back to you, a hundred fold.

The Black Moonstone of Borneo is a tektite which fell in a swarm during the Pleioscene Age.'

The Ancients believed that these stones which fell from the sky in a meteoric shower were holy. The Romans believed this and the Arabs and the Chinese and the Malaysians.

The holy stone, the Kaaba, at Mecca is one. There is another in Cyprus and another in Gibraltar. Holy healing stones from Heaven, bringing abundance in every way.

They are black, usually round or pear shaped, for coming through the earth's atmosphere and the outer surface is pitted like orange peel. In a mineral or expo you can buy them for as little as two pounds or four dollars. But if you are tempted to buy Moldavite which is a mixture of heavenly and earthly energy in combination, I'd say the energy of the simple tektite is far higher and purer!

Zeolite I referred to earlier is the only mineral which takes into itself. It absorbs illness from the land, animals and, of course, people. It has been known for thousands of years to clean the earth, and vets use it for healing animals. It is taken by mouth in solution after being crushed. Its form is hexagonal, and it is anti-cancerous and also has very good results in helping children who are autistic. Studies have been in place for over fifteen years in a research programme in Australia. Teams go to Japan and China after nuclear accidents, caused by tsunamis, or earthquakes, to heal the land. Zeolite is used in all Russian hospitals.

Aporting of minerals is common. They disappear and come back randomly. I believe they get reprogrammed to a higher frequency. Distance and continents travelled make no difference! When they are ready, they return and when they rejoin their fellow minerals, they are very hot where the others are cool.

During a crystal healing I was giving in USA, and in a heightened state. I placed the minerals on the chakras of the patient, each mineral corresponding to the colour of each chakra. So carnelian, red for the base, orange calcite for the second, citrine for the third, aventurine for the heart, turquoise for the throat,.lapis lazuli for the third eye and amethyst for the crown.

In the healing room were other large chunks of rose quartz, amethyst, clear quartz and apophyllite and as I watched, streams of energy from each flowed to the patient, joining with the energy of the minerals on the chakras of the patient. They activated or released energy when needed.

# 20

In the healing with crystals the colours of the minerals matched the chakras.

Colour is very important in healing for it is not only proven to be psychologically healing, but also physiologically healing too.

There are many colour healing kits, very beautiful and very expensive, but truly using crayons drawn on a piece of paper and applied to the area of the body which is sick is just as effective. Imagine there was a burn. It needs to be cooled, so use blue. Imagine there is a tumour and that needs to shrink, use violet.

Imagine that your heart feels a bit tired, use green to revive. The energy. Red is a bit too powerful, so leave it out. Visualize, as you are applying the paper with the relevant colout on the area, that your body is absorbing what it needs for its well being. Just as you do going into a supermarket, you will be drawn automatically to what your body needs, not with the conscious brain but automatically, in the true brain of the body, the gut. It will tell u,'aubergines would be good,' and then you look it up and discover that they are excellent if you have a deficiency in Vitamin B1,B6 and Potassium.

You will, of course, think if visualization alone can heal, the power of intention is so strong, do I really need even a paper with a coloured crayon on it? Well that depends on your spiritual advancement but a focus in the material dimension we are living in, is good.

A simple tool and of course coloured lights to use are available. I was in London years ago at a Science expo and there was a large tent where one could lie on a mat and be bathed in violet light. It was very soothing and healing In another room, at this expo, there was a. huge wooden violin-like instrument with strings on either side. The patient lay on top of it and two people, one on either side, played the strings and the reverberation went right through the spinal chord. It was a wonderful experience and it was used in Switzerlend as a healing tool for the mentally ill. Of course something like that would cost thousands of pounds, a unique instrument.

A colour healer who was also a theatre lighting man, devised his healing place where the colours moved in sequence in a darkened room to the accompaniment of soft music A. very healing and soothing experience, colour and sound in combination.

At the highest level of colour are the silver ray and the golden ray. Only very occasionally in my work have I met anyone who was on the Silver Ray. Most healers are on the violet.

The Silver is an octave above.

I like to simplify, for many people cannot afford expensive healing tools. At the end of every workshop and lecture, I always say the words, 'Simplify and Share.'

During a workshop in Singapore the same applied. Instead of an expensive pendulum, a needle and thread are just as effective.

The psychological effects of colour are well documented. Soft pastel shades are used for maternity words, instead of stark white.

In prisons, where violent inmates are housed, the walls are pink, the colour. With green, of the heart chakra, and the behaviour gentles.

Yellow is a great colour for children's study area. It invigorates the mind, helps with the homework, but should never be used in a bedroom, for it will interfere with sleep.

Lilac is soothing, creating tranquility. Green for a happy, healing room and red, never, for it can cause arguments in the home!

Warm Autumn tones are very relaxing for a family room.

For clothing, turquoise and peach are two good colours for TV presenters, turquoise especially for communication.

Black gets a bad press associating it with bereavement, but in my work, I have noticed a lot of sensitives wear black, for it shelters the person in a way. If a bright colour is used as an accessory, like emerald green, or scarlet, it's a good compromise.

White has impact always. I like it a lot in Mediterranean homes, a good cool colour against which the cushions can be as vivid as the geraniums which grow outside in profusion, or soft blue, like plumbago.

Orange makes us feel cheerful. Brown is grounding. Violet is dramatic and theatrical.

The more we use colour in our lives, the happier and richer we are!

Remember, green expands, violet contracts, so any tumour, lilac to violet clothing is good, never green but the green of Nature revives and re-energizes us, it is the colour of the heart chakra.

The three lower chakras are magnetic while the three highe, rare electric Green is the balancer, neither magnetic nor electric. Lunar people, who prefer night to day, suit electric colours best, and black white and silver.

# 21

As I described the beautiful musical healing 'violin, 'sound healing has always fascinated me. In Ubud, in Bali, a healer there gave my younger son and I sound healing. We lay on two adjacent mattresses with our heads at opposite ends, north south, south north. She sat in the middle playing the crystal bowls. We soon went into a higher plane. as she continued, for perhaps thirty minutes, sensing which were the chakras that needed healing in both. The sounds were beautiful, merging into each other, almost like a waterfall of sound. Once, many years ago, I had a vision of being in a white, soft, sheepskin garment, behind a waterfall in a small cave. To get to it, I'd had to traverse a wide chasm.

This experience with the crystal bowls felt much the same, as it took me to a different zone. We both felt very refreshed and almost, reborn at, the end of the session.

There were blue water lilies in a pond there in Ubud which I had never seen before.

I had heard of blue lilies in the Himalyas but I never saw them. They sound so beautiful.

The Gonalong gongs which I had heard in Brunei at weddings were also healing and almost hypnotic to listen to. These are made of brass ranging from small to large gongs and a group of men sit crosslegged on the carpets, striking their individual gongs on either side of the base which is like a giant bambo zylaphone where the drums are poised on strings.

The drumsticks, clad in soft leather, strike the gongs in harmony.

One of the loveliest sights in Brunei was when I attended an evening wedding on the Water Village. The bride, exquisitely dressed, in embroidered rich silks and jewelry waited in her bedroom on her throne waiting for the groom to arrive. We looked out across the water, sparkling with the lights of the harbour and the wedding boat came into view, candles lit at the prow, the gonalong players' music, wafting across the water. The groom dressed all in white, his long Arabic style gown and white songkok (a hat, a little like a small fez), such a dignified and romantic scene.

I was invited in to the room as a great privilege and saw the groom take his seat on the throne alongside that of his bride. The Imam conducted the service from the Koran.

It was very moving, and the sound of the gonalong always reminds me of that occasion.

In Sydney, taking part in a large expo, I heard an unearthly, pure sound and excusing myself, I hurried round the Conference Hall looking for the source of this magical sound.

There was a large group of people gathered around this booth, but looking over the shoulders I could see the beautiful healing chimes, some in natural wood, some varnished to a deeper colour, some painted brightly. The healer, a young woman had business cards and I hurried back to my table.

I ordered the natural wood, because it looked Japanese, Zen to me. The course was short and clear and

I incorporate the chimes into my healing the workshops have been held in USA Cyprus, UK, Singapore, Egypt and Dubai. German workmanship is in the making of the chimes and Australian wood is used for the base.

As they were first used in a workshop of healers, I was intrigued to get the feedback. All were enthusiastic. Some felt their headaches go. Others felt they could move more easily. Some felt they could run for miles but the most potent example of the effect of the chimes was someone who cried, years of suffering released. Whose face afterwards seemed ten years younger?

They are called elfin chimes and they do really feel otherworldly!

Once in USA near Canada I was staying with a fellow seer who lived near a wide wood. She had a flute and played it for the trees and the flute was made from one of the trees. An amazing resonance. I have heard the same in Dartmoor in South East England where they make harps and wind instruments from the local trees.

In total harmony, with the musician and the land.

In Sam ye ling in Scotland I heard the Tibetan monks play the wonderfully long horn which resonates with an extraordinarily deep note that thrills every cell in the body.

I played my chimes, as I wrote earlier, for the delight of the sheep, grazing, at the top of Glastonbury Tor!

**22**

Yoga has always been an important feature in my life as a teacher and as a student. Of Hatha and Raja yoga, Hatha, physical, Raja dealing with the subtler planes.

When I was in Brunei, I attended a yoga class run by an extraordinary Indian healer and teacher. Who was also a teacher of Physics. We practiced daily and he proposed I and others would study healing with him. Every day, I did massage with selected oils on a lovely lady who was in a wheelchair with arthritic joints. She followed a regimen of salt baths, daily massage, and a strict diet. After years she progressed to walking with a cane and finally, no cane, a wonderful thing to see.

While I could learn about oils and massage techniques and which foods were helpful in certain illnesses and which were detrimental, there was no way that any of us could emulate the resetting of shoulders and. limbs. A truly amazing healer I kept copious notes of the illnesses and the remedies. I still treasure that file.

The most unusual person I worked on, was a doctor, Indian, from the local hospital. He had a large soft mass at his Adam's apple. He had been tested for cancer and it was clear.

The healer would never go against medical opinion with tumours.

So I was given an elephant's molar to grind into a paste with a stone and water.

We looked at each other, the doctor and me, as if to say, 'Can't believe this!' I worked away with the stone and the molar, hard work to make the thin white paste. It was then applied to the soft mass and he was told to return every day for a fortnight At the end of the fortnight the mass had totally disappeared and the Adam's apple was normal. We were both amazed and asked why this was a cure.

'No one really knows for sure but it is only the molar that has this healing quality. We think it is because so much herbage is masticated by the molar that it is rich in healing energy.'

The doctor had not wanted surgery and believed in the ancient Indian medical practice of Ayurveda. Chinese ancient medical knowledge is very similar using herbs, flowers and plants to heal in harmony with Nature.

I was an apprentice for years and I still live my life in the Ayurvedic way. This is the science of life and is one of the four Vedas in ancient Hindu tradition.

Here are some of the remedies.

Headaches, including migraine / Cut a lemon in half and rub the cut edge round in circles over each temple several times. A teaspoonful of honey, licked slowly from a tea spoon will also help.

Arthritis, both kinds, osteo and rheumatoid. / Epsom salt baths three times a week. Ginger is the sovereign remedy. It is taken internally and applied externally.

Chop two inches of root ginger, peeled, and place in a teapot. Pour in boiling water.

Leave to infuse for five minutes. Drink one cup three times a day.

External usage / Massage the limb with any oil, almond, sunflower, olive. Meanwhile chop four inches of unpeeled root ginger in a pot with three inches of cold water and bring to the boil and simmer for ten minutes till the water is a rich yellow-orange colour. Apply with a face cloth wrung out as hot as possible, and place on the affected part, finally wrapping a towel over the face cloth and leave for twenty minutes. Do this on alternate days. If the person has a sensitive skin, perhaps fair haired or red haired, use less ginger so that the skin is not irritated.

Foods to avoid for arthritis / meat, tomatoes, oranges, any kind of shell food from the sea. Lemon juice daily is good, Nature's heal all.

For painful periods /Cinnamon bark tea. Three inches of cinnamon bark broken up and put in a teapot, cover with boiling water, infuse for five minutes and drink three cups a day.

To lower cholesterol / a clove of garlic bitten in half, swallowed down with two tablespoonfuls of apple cider vinegar, diluted with the equivalent amount of water.

Diabetes / blue berry tea, three cups daily.

These are common ailments for cancer use Zeolite. This I have learned subsequently from studying Ayurveda.

The oils to have at home.

Lavendar /for aiding sleep.

Nutmeg for arthritis / two or three drops in a teaspoonful of carrier oil, like olive. Massage round finer joints in circles.

Orange oil / my favourite, and which I always have. Burn two or three drops in a burner with a little water. This counteracts sadness, melancholy, for it releases the hormone in the part of the brain governing optimism and cheerfulness.

Rose or rose-geranium (cheaper than pure rose) /to help deal with grief, heals the emotional heart.

N.B.to retrain the body to install a good sleep pattern. Exercise vigorously before bed. Relax in a blood temperature bath. Boil five lettuce leaves in two inches of water. Simmer for five minutes and drink. Any kind of lettuce will do. Lettuces are well known in all cultures as a natural cure for sleeplessness. (Think of Peter Rabbit falling asleep in the lettuce patch!)

**23**

Loving flowers as we all do, it, felt like an extension in a way of the Ayurvedic way of life and I looked around for a system of study that would accommodate my busy life working as a seer and healer in many countries worldwide. I liked the energy of a school in New Jersey, USA and enrolled. The course was to take a year but because I was going between Cyprus and USA it took eighteen months, doing six modules each time I visited USA. It was such an interesting course, for in many ways, it blended with Ayurvedic teaching. For example Agrimony tea is taken to relieve negativity, Ayurvedically, and Agrimony is personified in flower essence training, as helpful for people who are cheerful on the outside but sad inwardly.

I have already described the love I have for the red, red lily, the Amayllis, which always blooms when an important event takes place in my family. It was love at first sight for me when I saw this in the Cameron Highlands in Malaysia so passionately red and triumphant a flower!

As part of the Flower Essence course, Dr. Bach, the British pioneer in this field, and his work was of course included as well as the additional healing of the flowers of the Northern Hemisphere and Alaska. Australian Bush remedies and European countries have their own remedies, from local plants and flowers

It was Dr. Bach's discovery that had most impact on me that if one was sick, the earth itself responds by bringing in wild flowers and plants needed to heal the condition in a six foot radius. In other words that the earth is sensitive to our needs and gives us the healing response, spontaneously.

Flower essences for emotional states, like fear, mimulus, peppermint for mental alertness, sage for wisdom, walnut for independence, rockrose for courage. So many and such a vast field of knowledge. As I wrote walnut, I remembered how I felt hostility to this oil and I said to the healer in Brunei, 'I don't like this oil.'

He said, 'There are many which I do not like. They are necessary for the healing of others. So get on with it!' A good response!

Orchids always seem a bit sinister to me, as if they are half belonging to the flora but also to the insect or even animal kingdom. But I love their beauty.

In the jungle of Borneo there were pitcher plants, which caught flies in the trap, cup- like plants.

I learned how to grow orchids in the air, with no earth. Line half a coconut with fibre. Place charcoal pieces in the fibre with crushed eggshells. Place the orchid plant within the coconut and suspend it from a tree or branch. From time to time add more eggshell. They bloom beautifully.

A rose which fills me with joy is the Damascus rose, a pale delicate pink, rather like a wild rose but bigger. The perfume is intoxicating and in the village of Agros in Cyprus, every home has these roses in the garden and products from them are made in the little factory. The name means Village of Roses.

Here is a true story, the implications of which I am still trying to work out!

After I finished the course in Flower Essences I contacted the leading expert in orchid essences who lives in Scotland in the West Coast. A healer in Singapore told me about him. He had studied orchid healing there.

So we were chatting about the course in USA and Australian Bush remedies and he said,

'I know you are sensitive. If I hold an orchid in my hand, can you please tune in and tell me what it's saying to you?'

I was happy to oblige.

'Wow! This plant is so powerful, it is almost black, and the energy is almost impossible to contain! It is Yang energy at the highest level!"

'Yes, he said 'that is exactly right and I'm not sure yet what kind of essence to make with it.' and he proceeded to tell me this story.

A very good friend of his, a Botanist, living in London, had a vivid dream that he was visited by a dark orchid, Who? Which? told him that he came from Africa and that his sister was in Japan. A white orchid was subsequently found in Japan, a perfect Yin match to the Yang from Africa.

How can a plant in Scotland communicate with a man in London to tell him where his sister is and where he came from originally. Plant life communicating with animal life (us) telepathically? The Nature Spirit within the plant reaching out for the furtherance of our knowledge of how little we know, no matter how much we have studied, only our toes in the water!

When the time came for my exam for the Diploma in Flower Essence Healing, the papers were sent to me in Cyprus. I sat at this desk for eleven hours, able to check from all the reference books and went to bed. In the morning I could not find a shred of text anywhere on the compute. Though I had saved as I went along.

Knowing that if I didn't do it all over again immediately,. I'd never do it again. In a roasting hot August I did another eleven hours outside in the garden, copied it to hard copy and sent it, registered to USA.

When in New Jersey I was in a park one day and I saw a creature I had never seen before. Big, like a large hedgehog and it followed me everywhere after my toes in sandals. A jogger stopped and said,

'Well I've never seen a groundhog do that before!'

The other animal that I have only seen in USA New York state is the Fisher cat. What a strange human wail it has. It is a badger type creature with a thirty kilometer beat and it is rare to see them, but you can certainly hear them!

**24**

In this period of time it seemed right to add Reiki healing to every. other kind I had studied This was gained in Harrogate in the North of England. This healing modality has evolved as practitioners add Reki to their own healing techniques.

It always seemed as if the East, philosophically and in spiritual practice felt right for me, not as a religion but a philosophy. As a Tibetan Buddhist I was not allowed to do hands on healing in a church but in a holistic centre, I did use spiritual hands on healing and loved the energy and the happiness of the people who received it.

In the visits to Harrow gate, the water in the hotel was amazing. It felt like champagne against the skin while showering. Only afterwards did I remember it was a spa during the eighteen hundreds, along with Bath in the south of England.

As a Reiki Master, I gave to healers I knew in Cyprus, the three levels, knowing they would not be able to leave the island or be able to afford the study. I could do this from my teaching, but there was disapproval from some who did not think the same way as I did. I am sure Dr. Usui gave the attunement to all the ships'. Captains at once and without repayment of any kind other than knowing that a healing modality was going out around the world.

I was given a lovely gift of a Reiki session from an American friend. She had set the atmosphere with soft lights, gentle music and I was delighted to lie down and close my eyes!

As I lay there I heard snapping fingers all round my head and I thought sleepily, this is a new experience in Reiki.

It was a wonderful healing I was given. When I sat up, I said,

'That was very interesting! I have never experienced snapping fingers as part of a Reiki session! I feel great, thank you!'

She looked at me and said,

'I wasn't snapping my fingers, there were only two of us in the room!'

I asked a friend who has excellent gifts if she had heard of this snapping.

'Yes,' she said,' My guides told me about this. It is to break up too much mental energy which has accumulated.'

I had been working very hard. It is a good technique to use when deadlines are causing tension in the head. A quick visit to the restroom to clear the energy in this way, will help a lot!.

# 25

Thinking that I should employ the opposite side of the brain, the cognitive, as well as the affective, I studied Neuro Linguistic Programming, N.L.P. in the South East of England.

It has helped many people to replace negative experiences with positive, and I am happy that I studied this field of healing. But it is not truly a fit for me, I think. It's the other side of my brain that has the most capacity for helping others.

Also with Psychometry, when an object is placed in the hand and sensitives can see the person who owned this or the place it came from, that does not really feel like a fir for me. I admire people immensely who do this with speed and accuracy and always tell them so!

Except for the time when I worked with the archaeologist in the family when I could clearly see the ships, the adornment of the Viking type men, but as with the visitation of the goddess Athena in her form as an owl, perhaps the two of us were working together in harmony, to bring forward this higher perception. Just as a group can manifest very high energy more than one. On his or her own.

I like to notice reoccurring numbers, angelic numbers, which tell us angels are close and that we are supported by them. It is comforting.

Today is Good Friday, in the Eastern calendar and the energy is sombre, so I will turn the energy to that of the animal kingdom.

# 26

Animals give us unconditional love. They heal us when we are sad, lying close to us till we heal. I believe they come back with souls and continue, after passing, just like the horses and Dylan the cat sitting on the back seat of the car in my last driving test. As I sobbed with relief over the steering wheel as the huge sergeant said, 'Congratulations! You will never have to sit another driving test in your life again.'

As he led me into the Sergeants' Mess where my driving instructor was sitting, he said,

'What would she be like, lads, if she'd failed?' The men were all sitting there, grinning, very military, short back and sides, and at their feet, beautiful Alsatian dogs. They were dog handlers. I felt the dogs' compassion as I drank the mug of strong sweet tea they gave me for shock. The driving instructor had been inspirational to me.

She was tiny and taught the men to drive tanks. She said,

'I never wanted anyone to pass as much as I did you.' And she cried too!

Performance anxiety is a terrible thing making you see a red light and think, it's a trap and drive straight through it!

I had a dog once. He adopted me and the students when I was teaching in Glasgow. He walked in crocodile with us to the classroom and lay down at my desk. We fed him daily and then he was spotted as the head teacher looked through the little window. We called him, Jason. He was with me for a while until I was told by the landlord he would have to go. A loving family adopted him. He still has a place in my heart.

Cats have been very important in my family's life as I have mentioned earlier.

Aphrodite, Domino, Murphy, Dylan and Merry. They adapted well to life in the jungle, after Scotland, living to late old age, in their twenties.

Horses feel very close to their masters. I have been told of horses, completely well, who have died of broken hearts when their masters have passed away.

One such was Satan an ungovernable horse about to be put down for his vicious temper, but one man rescued him, and from that moment, they were inseparable, but only his master could ride him.

Working in a saw mill he had an accident to his arm. His wife asked Satan if she could ride him to get to the doctor. On this occasion, he rode as fast as he could. The moment the man died, the horse died. Devotion.

There are many stories and legends of noble dogs who wait patiently for their masters to return, often for the rest of their lives.

If we have this strong love for the animal kingdom, we become vulnerable through love, unable to bear the loss of wild creatures in Bush fires, or dogs left behind by their owners to roam motorways, always looking for their family. In contrast we can seem almost inferior to the animal kingdom with their unconditional love and loyalty.

They love us, protect us, heal us, lift our energy with joy and comradeship. We owe them so much!

A few years ago I went on a Horse Whispering course, in Sussex, UK. The herd of horses was there with the owner and teacher. She explained that the horses would do the choosing and that they would be the teachers. I looked at them all as I stood in the corner of the field, where they had gently corralled me. Jacob was a very large horse, white and he was the leader and the first. I held out my hand, flat, as I had done when we had riding lessons when the children were small, and Jacob gave me a gentle nip.

'A one woman horse,' his owner laughed.

One by one they came and checked me out, with curiosity, ambled off. And two horses remained with me.

'They are the youngest horses in the herd,' I was told.

One was chestnut and the other a gypsy cob, black and white, and with an untidy fringe!

I was taught to put my fingertips on their chest and they would go backwards, and when I walked away, looking over my shoulder, they would follow me At the end of the day, I felt so close to them and when the chestnut leant against me, closed his eyes and fell asleep in my arms, I felt I had been given a most precious gift. Leaving the two and waving as they stood at the gate, watching me go, I had a lump in my throat. Their picture is on the screen in my sitting room.

# 27

In London I was sitting at my table at an expo, and Dave walked past looking at the Encaustic wax cards I use at the end of each session for the client to have visual confirmation of the purely channeled oral session. and he said, 'These would blend very well with Sand Readings. Come when you are free and I will teach you.'

Sand is how it was taught to me but getting the right sand is difficult Sometimes it goes into clumps or it has tiny stones. Eventually I found the right kind as I drove past builders and asked if I could buy a kilogram. They kindly gave me some but wanted to know why I needed it. They thought it was for art, which it is, in a way.

A round tray is needed, with a rim of maybe one inch. An aluminum large cake or pizza shape will do that can be bought for baking at any supermarket.

I now use flour or talcum powder instead of sand for they hold the shapes that form Perfectly, and when I travel it is not easy to find sand or even carry it, from country to country.

As you sit opposite the client, you tell them to play in the 'sand'till they feel ready to stop. As you look down you will see that the circle has two halves to the right affective, emotional, to the left cognitive, mental. Closest to you is the age of the person from youngest age to the opposite edge, late old age.

If the base is showing through, that is a very important aspect of their life. There will be mountains, numbers perhaps, faces, symbols, designs and patterns from different cultures.

If the right side is higher and remember the imaginary line is longitudinal through the circle, you know the person's present state is more the emotional, than the cerebral and vice versa if the left is higher than the right. As you read the shapes you will feel the solar plexus altering, and the breathing changing, exactly the same as if you are looking into water. If, at the far away rim from yourself, there is a wavy line, you know the person is mediumistic.

At a workshop in Shanghai I used sand readings for each and had the group see what they could see for each other. It was fascinating from, 'Oh I couldn't do this!' to 'Oh, look 1 there is a capital T. He must have a strong connection with you.' How quickly they could see!

We then used the Encaustic wax for a Life Soul Path for each. This technique was first shown to me in Sydney. In my Life Soul Path, (you can only have one done, obviously, for it is for your whole life,) the aspects of my life clearly show and I look at it daily.

The client chooses five colours of wax lozenges from the many. A waxed card is used for the picture which will form. On the Encaustic wax iron, an ordinary one doesn't work for I tried it once, you apply the five colours chosen in horizontal stripes across the iron.

Keep the iron turned up towards you, so they don't merge too much. Then the iron is turned over and glides twice from the bottom of the card to the top. Then it is left to cool as the pictures form. They may be incredibly exact, as if you had drawn them with a pen or a fine squirrel hair paint brush. They are left to dry and put inside a cellophane envelope. to protect them.

In that workshop, the group saw that each participant's sand, and wax, reading were telling the same story, like looking into a room through two different windows.

Water is a great conductor, sand also, and wax, denser than both.

In Hong Kong I was amused to see a seer reading lipstick traces from a paper napkin.

Traditionally, in the Middle East coffee grounds are used for scrying and tea leaves in the West. And people have read the clouds and flames in the fire from the beginning of time!

# 28

This would be incomplete without the meetings of the Star People There are so many sightings of spaceships that I don't need to describe my sightings of them. In Scotland.

In the South West of England an American lady came to visit me. As I opened the faculty I heard the words from my guides, "she is from the stars." As the session proceeded more and more information came about her reason for being on the Earth, as a healer and catalyst for change. It was a very long and intense session. She told me no one had been able to see that before. She gave me her phone number and we kept in touch over the years.

Two days after this meeting, synchronicity at work, I was at an expo and a tall, handsome young man came straight to my table, totally bypassing everyone else. I thought this was odd. Normal, and correct practice in my opinion, is that people should sense the energies of many before they are called by the energy of the person they are meant to see.

He sat down and said, 'You are the one I was told I had to see.'

I thought this was odd and asked him what he meant, but he shook his head.

The session began and again I was told, "This is a star person."

He nodded, and the session began. Towards the end I said, 'I am seeing the Controller.'

He stopped me and said, 'You are seeing too much. Please stop now.'

It was the Controller who had sent him to me and I wonder to this day, how he could see me. He said he knew many others in South Africa, star people like himself but none in UK.

I quickly made a phone call to the first from two days previously, to ask if I could give him her phone number. And she agreed. He was given details about food and diet and that he should live on a higher elevation and finally I gave him a Moldavite to help balance him. Since then I have encountered them in Skyros, USA, Australia, a few, Malaysia. Most recently, USA again, perhaps fifteen in all. When I ask my friends on this path, 'Have you met the Star people? They shake their heads. Someday I will know the answer. They are very intelligent, often in government and many are healers simultaneously and they all love the arts and beauty.

# CONCLUSION

My story is ended for now. I was told to write everything I knew for the seers and sensitives coming behind. I've used this time of lockdown for I know the road goes on from here and I will add to this in the future.

Each of us is different and our gifts emerge in different ways, no better, or worse than.

To my grandmother, Anne Gavin, an extraordinary woman I believe, from whom I inherited my gifts, I honour you and all those others who would have kept their gifts hidden, for safety, in the times and cultures in which they lived.

From my voyage of life as a seer, I wish you, 'Bon Voyage!'

Anne Austin
Kallepeia
CYPRUS
April 24th 2020

Printed in the United States
By Bookmasters